W.B. YEATS

A BEGINNER'S GUIDE

FRANK STARTUP

Series Editors
Rob Abbott and Charlie Bell

Hodder & Stoughton

A MEMBER OF THE HODDER HEADLINE GROUP

Orders: please contact Bookpoint Ltd, 130 Milton Park, Abingdon, Oxon OX14 4SB. Telephone: (44) 01235 827720, Fax: (44) 01235 400454. Lines are open from 9.00–6.00, Monday to Saturday, with a 24-hour message answering service. Email address: orders@bookpoint.co.uk

British Library Cataloguing in Publication Data
A catalogue record for this title is available from The British Library

ISBN 0 340 84646 1

First published 2002
Impression number   10 9 8 7 6 5 4 3 2 1
Year   2007 2006 2005 2004 2003 2002

Cover photo from Hulton-Deutsch/Corbis

Typeset by Transet Limited, Coventry, England.
Printed in Great Britain for Hodder & Stoughton Educational, a division of Hodder Headline Plc, 338 Euston Road, London NW1 3BH by Cox & Wyman, Reading, Berks

CONTENTS

Contents

How to use this book

The *Beginner's Guide* series aims to introduce readers to major writers of the past 500 years. It is assumed that readers will begin with little or no knowledge and will want to go on to explore the subject in other ways.

BEGIN READING THE AUTHOR

This book is a companion guide to Yeats's major works, it is not a substitute for reading the books themselves. It would be useful if you read some of the works in parallel, so that you can put theory into practice. This book is divided into sections. After considering how to approach the author's work and giving a brief biography, we go on to explore some of his main writings and themes before examining some critical approaches to the author. The survey finishes with suggestions for further reading and possible areas of further study.

HOW TO APPROACH UNFAMILIAR OR DIFFICULT TEXTS

Coming across a new writer may seem daunting, but do not be put off. The trick is to persevere. Much good writing is multi-layered and complex. It is precisely this diversity and complexity which makes literature rewarding and exhilarating.

Literary work often needs to be read more than once and in different ways. These ways can include: a leisurely and superficial reading to get the main ideas and narrative; a slower more detailed reading focusing on the nuances of the text and concentrating on what appear to be key passages; and reading in a random way, moving back and forth through the text to examine such things as themes, narrative or characterization.

In complex texts it may be necessary to read in short chunks. When it comes to tackling difficult words or concepts it is often enough to guess in context on the first reading, making a more detailed study using a dictionary or book of critical concepts on later reading. If you prefer to look up unusual words as you go along, be careful that you do not disrupt the flow of the text and your concentration.

VOCABULARY

You will see that KEYWORDS and unfamiliar words are set in **bold** text. These words are defined and explained in the glossary to be found at the back of the book. This book is a tool to help you appreciate a key figure in literature. We hope you enjoy reading it and find it useful.

✳ ✳ ✳ *SUMMARY* ✳ ✳ ✳

To maximize the use of this book:

- Read the author's work.

- Read it several times in different ways.

- Be open to innovative or unusual forms of writing.

- Persevere.

Rob Abbott & Charlie Bell

Why Read Yeats Today?

1

A PASSIONATE AND ORIGINAL MIND

To read Yeats's poetry is to enter the mind of a highly original writer who recorded, in detail and in wonderfully vivid imagery, the events of his life and his impressions of the world around him. It is also to read the history of Ireland from the late nineteenth century until the outbreak of the Second World War. During this period, following the horrors of the Great Famine, republican and nationalist movements grew from a determination to throw off British rule. This movement culminated in the partitioning of Ireland and the early days of the Republic. Through it all, Yeats was an important public figure, a man who believed passionately that national identity is rooted in national culture, a man who admired the bravery of the revolutionaries, but who continued to have misgivings about political movements.

A DEVELOPING VOICE

Many of Yeats's early poems are beautiful in their depiction of a legendary Ireland, a Celtic mythology of heroes and supernatural beings. Yeats weaves this mythical past together with the historical present to show the grandeur and beauty he perceived in those around him. The love poetry is passionate and yearning, and it is impossible for the reader not to be swept up in Yeats's world and poetic vision. As Yeats grows older and experience whittles away the enthusiasm and hope of youth, the poetry changes in tone, although many of the old themes remain. Elements of resignation, anger and disillusionment begin to temper the passionate optimism of youth. It is an exciting journey into the intellectual and emotional life of an extraordinary man living in extraordinary times, seeing how experience hones the perceptions of innocence.

A WIDE RANGE OF STYLES

Yeats's first poems appeared in the late nineteenth century and he continued writing until his death in 1939, aged 74. He began writing, therefore, towards the end of the Victorian era when Browning and Tennyson were still alive and he finished writing in the world of Eliot, Auden and Pound. The influence of the Romantic movement and the Pre-Raphaelites is clear in the early poetry (around 1886–1910), which is magical, full of mystery and the supernatural. **Lyric poetry** and ballads draw on ancient Irish legends and folklore, and the poet inhabits his work as, among other figures, 'The Lover'.

Early poems deal with nature and the beauty of the land, such as 'The Lake Isle of Innisfree' and with romantic devotion to a loved one, such as,

> **KEYWORDS**
>
> Lyrical poetry: originally, short poems intended to be sung to the accompaniment of a lyre. A lyric is now the name for any short poem expressing personal feeling.
>
> Satire: drawing attention to human failings, the ridiculous and the hypocritical by ridiculing them.
>
> Elegy: a poem of meditation, sad and reflective, usually concerned with the theme of death or having as it subject someone who has died.

'He Wishes for the Cloths of Heaven'. The poems of his middle (around 1910–1926) and last (around 1927–1939) periods record experiences of disillusionment and loss, reactions to and thoughts upon current events, the nature of love and the approach of death. The tone of the poetry becomes sterner, less idealistic. There are **satires** and **elegies**, and the poetry becomes less wistful and romantic, more physical and muscular.

There is an astonishing range of imagery drawn from Irish myth, Eastern religions, classical legend, Christianity and the various occult systems which fascinated Yeats. Images are also drawn from across the canon of English and Irish writers. These sources are woven into his presentation of the physical, tangible world around him, drawing the spiritual and the physical, the seen and the unseen, the past and the present, the intuitive and the empirical into a whole unified by the figure of the poet himself. Yeats, like all great writers, enables us by his use of language and his creation of vivid imagery to see ourselves, our past and our world through other eyes and from a new perspective.

RECORD OF AN ERA

Yeats wrote during one of the most volatile periods of his country's history, and his poetry captures this. The defeat of the Irish Home Rule Bill, the fall of Parnell and the founding of the Fenian movement, in its various forms led to the uprising of 1916 and, eventually, to the Civil War which ended in partition. In the world beyond this struggle, Yeats saw the start and finish of the First World War, and the events in Europe, which culminated in the beginning of the Second World War. Yeats writes about historical events and personalities vividly. There are elegies to dead heroes and tributes to revolutionaries, tempered by misgivings about the nature of politics and the need for something more.

As an Irishman attempting to establish an Irish National Theatre, he was at the centre of Ireland's cultural and political life, where his circle included soldiers, revolutionaries, poets, playwrights, politicians and Anglo-Irish aristocrats. By the time of partition, Yeats was an important public figure, respected and admired. He was a senator in the first Irish parliament, and a poet awarded a Nobel Prize for literature. To read Yeats is to be placed in the middle of a particular place at a particular time and to experience it as vividly as we experience Dickens's London, Hardy's Wessex or Wordsworth's Lakes.

RANGE OF SUBJECT MATTER

The range of themes in Yeats's writing – poetry, prose and drama – is immense, and offers illumination of our own conditions and circumstances. The relationship between citizen and country, heritage and culture is explored in a variety of ways, from the attempt to find a unifying mythology in the early poems to the reflections upon the nature and the end of politics in his later work. Experiences of love, requited and, very movingly, unrequited, are explored throughout the works. The struggle to make sense of experience, to find unity and meaning is central, and Yeats conducts this in several ways, most notably in the occult and mystical system expounded in his book *A Vision* and through the metaphorical and symbolic systems of his poetry. The supernatural permeates his work, as Yeats searches for patterns and cycles in his own experience and through history. Yeats also writes about the art and the purposes of poetry, the struggle to find inspiration and expression.

AUTOBIOGRAPHY

The first edition of Yeats's collected works appeared in 1908 and represented a reorganization and rewriting of material that Yeats was to continue throughout his life. Yeats spent much time rearranging and re-editing his work for this edition and throughout subsequent editions. Indeed, he also revised his essays, his collections of fiction and even his letters before publication. He sought to leave a body of work which would present his life, his experiences, his thoughts, his development as a poet and his growth as a human being, as an organic whole.

He was writing not just for his contemporaries, but for the future, trying to present, in the words of John Unterecker, 'the total experience of a man, a total experience, shaped through art, into a form less perishable that flesh' *A Reader's Guide to W. B. Yeats*, Thames and Hudson, 1959).

To read Yeats is to gain a picture, as complete as may be possible, of the experience of another life and mind.

✷ ✷ ✷ *SUMMARY* ✷ ✷ ✷

- Yeats is a great writer whose use of language and imagery is original and moving.

- Yeats records the spirit and events of his time vividly and evocatively.

- Yeats presents a picture of a poet's total experience, allowing us to share the development of another mind and spirit.

How to Approach Yeats

2

THE POEMS

The *Collected Poems* are at the centre of Yeats's work and are very rewarding when read chronologically, as you would a prose work or an autobiography. Most of us come to individual poets by finding examples of their work in anthologies and, if we like them, looking for others. Yeats can, of course, be 'dipped into' but, given the deliberate cohesiveness of his work, the way in which images and symbols are used to unite ideas and themes, and the ways in which these themes and ideas are developed across the course of a life's work, reading the poems in the sequence presented to you is best.

READING POEMS

Although it is recommended that you read the collected poems as a whole and in sequence, you will still, of course, be dealing with individual poems and you will have to approach them as you would any individual poem. Reading Yeats aloud is a good idea, even though you may get stared at on trains! Sound is very important to the reading of any poem and reading aloud will help you to understand the techniques of rhythm, rhyme, tone and diction employed by the poet at different times and for different purposes.

Apart from this suggestion, the usual advice for reading poetry effectively applies. Read through the poem several times, trying to determine the poet's mood and tone.

* Establish what the poem's subject is – what is it about?

* Ask yourself what the purpose of the poem is. Is it telling a story? Is it primarily descriptive? Does it put forward a point of view or argument?

* Is there a discernible meaning?

* Try to discover patterns of rhyme or rhythm, alliteration or assonance, and see how they contribute to the mood of the poem.

* Look for the descriptive devices, the metaphors and similes employed by the poem, and try to see how they convey meaning or enhance impression.

IMAGES

As you read on through the poems, keep a note of recurring images and themes. Become aware of how they are used and of the different ways in which they are explored and developed across a series of poems, across each separate book of poems and across the collected poems as a whole.

Much of Yeats's imagery is drawn from mythology or from different mystical systems and the later poetry draws imagery from the system or pattern of reality which Yeats describes in *A Vision*. Yeats, however, wanted to be understood. He was careful not to make the appreciation of his poetry dependent upon having read his prose or his plays, although, each does contribute to the whole, and understanding is deepened by a study of the whole.

THE SECOND COMING

The Second Coming is one of Yeats's most famous poems, written in 1919 and included in the collection *Michael Robartes and the Dancers*. It draws its imagery from Yeats's developing theories concerning cycles of history and the symbols he used to depict them in what was to become his book *A Vision*. Although a reading of that book will help to fix the poem's ideas and images within the system, not having read *A Vision* does not make the poem unintelligible. When we read:

> *Turning and turning in the widening gyre*
> *The falcon cannot hear the falconer;*
> *Things fall apart; the centre cannot hold...*

we do not need to understand the complexities of the systems of gyres to appreciate the image of a falcon spiralling in ever-widening circles away from the falconer to the point where control is lost. The rest of the poem, suggesting that a period of history dominated by the principles of Christianity is about to give way to its opposite, is symbolized by the flight of the falcon and is clear in its own context.

PROSE

Much of the prose aside from *A Vision* is gathered in three collections which are relatively easy to find: *Essays and Introductions*, *Mythologies* and *Autobiographies*. *Mythologies* gathers together *The Celtic Twilight* and *The Secret Rose* with the 1917 *Per Amica Sileantia Lunae*. Other fiction, such as *John Sherman*, will have to be sought elsewhere (see the Further Reading section). *Essays and Introductions* and *Autobiographies* contain essays and prose other than fiction which will be of interest to the reader of the poetry.

The prose is best read alongside the poetry, rather than as a prologue or an epilogue. Thus, *The Secret Rose*, published in 1897, should be read as an accompaniment to the poetry of the period, helping to illuminate Yeats's development as an artist in that period. Keep these volumes alongside the collected poetry and read them with the poems.

As this is a short guide aimed at providing an introduction for readers unfamiliar with much of Yeats's work and ideas, a thorough analysis of *A Vision* is neither appropriate nor possible. A reading of *A Vision* is recommended not, at this stage, for a thorough working knowledge of the phases of the moon, their opposites and the arcane workings of the gyres, but more for a general picture of the sort of system that Yeats envisaged. A copy, handy for reference, is all that is needed at this stage.

AUTOBIOGRAPHICAL PROSE

Applying the chronological principle to this writing is not so easy. The *Reveries Over Childhood and Youth* deals, obviously, with the poet's early life but was written in 1914 when his account of his childhood was coloured by experiences and hindsight. The same applies to Yeats's memories of *Four Years: 1887–1891*, and the deaths of Parnell and Synge. Again, it is recommended that these pieces are read as they occur, in the order in which his works are dated, as an accompaniment to the poetry. If you wish to read them – and can find them – the Senate speeches can be read in the same way. The letters, which will eventually run through 12 volumes (published by Oxford University Press, under the general editorship of John Kelly, Volumes 1–3 are currently in print), should possibly be reserved for later, although there is an excellent one-volume collection of correspondence with Maud Gonne.

DRAMA

The plays manifest a different expression of the ideas and beliefs that are contained in the poems. Yeats's early intention was to create a theatre for Ireland and he considered his plays to be like mystery plays in tone, structure and presentation, giving evidence of a hidden world, a reality beyond the material here and now. These plays, based on the occult, on Irish legends and interpretations of nationalism, give way to the plays of Yeats's middle period which primarily reflect the idea of masks and opposites of personality. The later plays not only experiment with other forms, such as Japanese Noh drama, but also, like the poems, return to earlier themes and explore them differently, in accordance with the symbolic syntheses that Yeats found in later life. Seeing the plays in performance is the best way to appreciate them, but, since you will probably read them rather than see them, a commentary on their staging and presentation is recommended (see Further Reading).

＊ ＊ ＊ SUMMARY ＊ ＊ ＊

- Read Yeats's writings, as far as possible, in chronological order.

- Read the poetry in sequence, as you would a prose autobiography.

- Read the poetry aloud and apply to your readings of individual pieces the same questions that you would ask about any individual poem.

- Be aware of recurring themes, images, symbols and correspondences.

- Read the prose and plays that you select alongside the poetry, not separately from it.

- Do not get hung up on *A Vision*.

- Read those plays you select with a commentary to help you to visualize their presentation on stage.

Biography, Background and Influences

3

Before we begin to look at Yeats's work, we need to know something of the world and the circumstances which shaped it. This is particularly important since the events of Yeats's life, his friends, his lovers, his relations and the places in which he lived are so central to his writing.

BIRTH AND CIRCUMSTANCES

William Butler Yeats was born in Dublin on 13 June 1865. His father, John Butler Yeats, was a barrister who had an additional income from inherited estates in County Kildare. Yeats's mother, Susan Pollexfen, came from Sligo in the west of Ireland where her family owned various companies. Yeats's sister Susan was born in 1866, and there were three more children to follow: two brothers and a sister. One of the brothers, however, died in 1873.

LONDON, DUBLIN AND SLIGO

Despite the middle-class trappings, Yeats's childhood was by no means conventional. His father wanted to become a painter and in 1867 he moved his growing family to London. Not only did he surrender his income as a barrister, the income from his lands in Kildare began to decrease. He was not a practical man and he did not know how to manage money well. The family drifted into genteel poverty. Susan and the children frequently travelled back to Sligo when money was unusually tight, in order to stay with her family. On these occasions, Yeats would wander off on his own, dreaming and walking around the countryside and talking to the locals, listening to their stories. Gradually the income from Kildare dried up and, in 1881, the Yeats family moved back to Dublin. By this time, Yeats had spent four years at the Godolphin school in Hammersmith, West London.

EDUCATION

Yeats had not been happy at school in Hammersmith, where he had been teased and bullied for his dreamy manner and his Irish accent. He found various strategies to avoid this ill-treatment, the most successful of which was learning how to best impress others, to adopt façades which would keep tormentors away. In 1881, he was taken out of this school and placed for a further three years in the High School, Dublin, where he discovered a great interest in poetry. From there, he went to Dublin's Metropolitan School of Art, which was where he decided that he wanted to be a poet.

FATHER'S INFLUENCE

As a man who loved art so much that he was prepared to sacrifice a potentially comfortable, secure life to pursue it, John Butler Yeats was not going to push his eldest son into business or commerce. He encouraged his son's love of poetry and made sure that his children were brought up in an atmosphere of enlightenment and culture, in which reading, discussion and self-expression were valued. He seems not to have worried that his son was unlikely to pass the entrance examination for the prestigious Trinity College, instead encouraging him to find his own voice and his own interests. Yeats's father read to him, argued with him, and introduced him to different theories of art. John Butler Yeats's father was an atheist whose political inclinations were nationalist: his mother's family was quietly religious, and its political inclinations lay in the direction of unionism. Yeats grew up in an atmosphere where ideas and art were very important, his father even advising him that regular employment would be a barrier to creativity and should be avoided.

IRISH HERITAGE

In his twenties, with all the advantages that a liberal and open-minded upbringing had given him, Yeats met an ex-**Fenian** named John

> ## KEYWORD
>
> Fenian: a movement which began in the late eighteenth century in America and was named after the Fianna, warriors from Irish legend. It advocated the immediate overthrow of British rule in Ireland, by force if necessary.

O'Leary, who interested him in the cause of Irish Nationalism and this led him to questions of Irish identity.

Yeats began to translate Irish writing into English, and he became fascinated by the ancient Irish legends. It was perhaps the wide-ranging intellectual freedom and liberality of his upbringing that made Yeats shy away from the stridencies of political nationalism. He concentrated upon trying to draw attention to the cultural heritage which was to be found in the ancient stories of heroes and magic. Yeats was to express the opinion that his work in reviving an Irish heritage was as important for Ireland as the work of those involved in nationalist politics.

THE OCCULT

In 1885, Yeats helped to found the Dublin Hermetic Society and an interest in mysticism and magic, which would last throughout his life, was first given open expression. He joined **Theosophist** societies in Ireland and in England.

Yeats attended seances and read widely the mystical literature of other cultures or belief-systems, such as Buddhism and Judaism. In

KEYWORDS

Theosophy: a generic term for mystical philosophies which say that a knowledge of God can be achieved through such means as direct intuition, spiritual ecstasy or a progression through rites and rituals.

1890, he joined the Order of the Golden Dawn, a secret society with initiation rites and secret magical practices. The society believed that, through ritual and ceremony, understanding of the universe could be achieved. The sense of ritual and symbolic importance in the revelation of truth was never to leave Yeats. His involvement with the magical and mysterious, however, did not blunt his recognition that there were different kinds of knowledge. His questions, his desire for evidence of a more empirical kind, led to his breaking with the London Theosophical Society and much later, in 1913, he joined the Society for Psychical Research, devoted to finding scientific explanations of and evidence for the apparently paranormal.

MAUD GONNE

Yeats first met Maud Gonne in 1889 and it changed his life and work forever. Physically striking – nearly six feet (1.8 m) tall with a profusion of golden-brown hair and a complexion which reminded Yeats of apple blossom – she was also an intelligent, passionate and deeply unconventional young woman. Maud hated the English and the British Empire and she turned her back on a privileged upbringing to become a revolutionary, campaigning vigorously for the Irish National Party and committing herself wholeheartedly to the cause of nationalism.

Yeats proposed marriage to Maud Gonne for the first time in 1891, only to be refused. She wanted his friendship, she wanted him to write poems and plays for her, but marriage to Yeats was not what she wanted. Her unconventionality extended to her personal relationships. She had already had two children by a French journalist, Lucien Millevoye; there was a son who died and a daughter, Iseult, born in 1894. In 1903, Maud

Gonne married the soldier and republican John MacBride. They had a son, Sean, but they separated two years after their marriage. Yeats continued to propose to Maud and to be refused. Nevertheless what she and her presence symbolized for him was to be one of the abiding themes of his work. Later, he was to propose marriage to Iseult and, again, be rejected.

LADY AUGUSTA GREGORY

In 1894, Yeats met the second of the four women who were so important in his life and work. Her name was Augusta Gregory, the widow of a colonial governor, and her estate at Coole Park in County Galway was to be a summer retreat for Yeats for many years. They shared an interest in the Irish heritage, manifested in Yeats's Irish Literary Revival. While she lent him money so that he could give up the journalism with which he had been scraping a living and concentrate upon his real work, he encouraged her to write stories, plays and her own translations of Irish myths and legends. It was through Augusta that Yeats met great Irish writers such as George Moore and George Bernard Shaw. She was instrumental in the forming of the Irish National Theatre, so close to Yeats's heart. Their relationship was characterized by great respect and affection. He always called her 'Lady Gregory' and she called him 'Willie'. She listened to him and encouraged him, supported him and gave him respite at Coole when it was needed. At Coole Park, Yeats found links to a different past – stately, noble and representing connections to a continuous artistic and cultural tradition.

OLIVIA SHAKESPEAR

At around the same time that he met Lady Gregory in London, Yeats also met the woman with whom he was to have his first sexual affair. Olivia Shakespear was a writer of plays and short stories and she was also interested in spiritualism. She was married to a solicitor who was much older than she and the attraction between herself and Yeats was virtually instantaneous. The relationship was not consummated sexually until a year after they met, thanks, in part, to Yeats's idealistic views of women and his lack of self-confidence. Although Yeats asked

Olivia to run away with him, the idea was far from practical given his lack of money and her situation and the affair ended in 1897.

ABBEY THEATRE

One element of Yeats's vision for an Irish Literary Revival, as part of the Celtic heritage, was an Irish theatre presenting Irish plays by Irish playwrights on Irish themes. With the great help of Lady Gregory and the active support of the artistic community, the Abbey Theatre in Dublin was opened in 1904. Plays that had been put on in halls around the country could now be presented at a permanent home for Irish theatre. Finance was raised, and Yeats managed the theatre from the time of its opening until 1910. The theatre's fortunes, however, were to run far from smoothly, and this was a contributory factor to the changes in tone of Yeats's work.

THE CELTIC TWILIGHT

In 1893, a collection of stories and poems carrying the title *The Celtic Twilight* seemed to sum up the mood and feeling of Yeats's work. The collection was dreamy and wistful, drawn from Irish folklore and embodying elements of Eastern and Christian, as well as Celtic, mythology. Yeats's interests in the occult lent the poems an esoteric symbolism which, along with references to obscure folk figures and spirits from ancient lore, meant that footnotes and explanations had to be provided. This, the early period of Yeats's writing, began, from the beginning of the new century, to give way to something else, something darker and this was reflected in the increasing spareness of his style.

DISILLUSIONMENTS

Love

Maud Gonne's repeated refusals to marry Yeats, her marriage to John MacBride and her preference for political action over the creation of a shared heritage to forge a cultural identity for Ireland, led to a change in the tone of Yeats's love poetry. His love for her was still expressed, but it was now tinged with pain and with a new knowledge and understanding of the real nature of their relationship.

Politics

Politics, too, disillusioned Yeats. After **Parnell**'s disgrace and subsequent death in 1891, there seemed to be a vacuum in Irish politics. The hope held out by Parnell's work had been thoroughly squashed.

It was in this period that the various Gaelic associations were established in order to bolster pride in Irish sport or language and it was in this climate that Yeats began his literary societies and the Irish National Theatre. He was a nationalist, but less interested in the mechanics of Home Rule than in the establishment of an Irish national identity and voice.

Yeats found the language and the attitudes of the political nationalists too violent and urgent. He was appalled by what he saw as Maud Gonne's rashness in throwing herself into, what were becoming called, the 'struggles'. Yeats joined the Irish Republican Brotherhood which fought for Home Rule and evolved into the IRA. However, he became disillusioned with the machinery, factions and in-fighting of revolutionary politics.

During the riots in Dublin in 1897, when protests about the celebration of Queen Victoria's Jubilee led to the death of an elderly woman and the wounding of around 200 people, Yeats physically prevented Maud Gonne from participating. Her response the next morning, was to raise bail for all the protesters

KEY FACTS

Parnell
Charles Stewart Parnell was a political leader who, as an Irish MP at Westminster, fought tirelessly and cleverly for Irish rights. He won tremendous victories with regard to the ownership of land in Ireland and was very close to achieving a Home Rule Bill when his adulterous love affair with Mrs Kitty O'Shea became public. The Catholic Church attacked him and Parnell was forced out of public life, dying a year later. To appreciate the feeling of trauma caused by the fall of Parnell, read the account of the Christmas dinner in Chapter One of James Joyce's *Portrait of the Artist as a Young Man*.

Home Rule
Many times the aim of Home Rule for Ireland, free from the British, seemed within grasp. However events such as the fall of Parnell and the outbreak of the First World War in 1914 saw it shelved or set back. In 1913, the Ulster Unionists, protestants who supported the crown and who feared marginalization in a Catholic republic, set up the Ulster Volunteers to resist Home Rule. Other organizations, such as Sinn Fein and the Irish Citizen Army, were formed in the south to fight for Home Rule.

who had been imprisoned. Yeats was, nonetheless, deeply impressed by the sacrifices made by the insurgents of the Easter 1916 uprising, which saw the ringleaders – including John MacBride – executed by the British.

The Theatre

The Abbey Theatre did not have a smooth run. As manager, Yeats supervized the finances and running of the theatre, and this took a tremendous amount of time. On top of this, he had to face criticism from various sources about some of the plays that were staged. Some of the objections to plays were made on religious grounds, others for political reasons. The opening of Synge's *Playboy of the Western World* was greeted with such a violent response that police had to be called to the theatre. A play written to awaken sensibilities had instead aroused prejudices and Yeats came to feel that a philistine public was almost wilfully missing the point.

Culture

The behaviour of Irish audiences, the responses which showed lack of understanding or even of the will to understand, was put into perspective during a visit to Italy with Lady Gregory and her son. Yeats drew unflattering comparisons between public attitudes to art in Ireland and Italy. This was exacerbated when Lady Gregory's nephew offered his collection of paintings to Dublin and found his offer indifferently received. Again, for Yeats, this was indicative of the lack of appreciation shown for art and culture. Each of these factors contributed to the close of the 'Celtic Twilight' period and the beginning of a new acerbity and directness in Yeats's poems.

GEORGIE-HYDE LEES

Bertha Georgie Hyde-Lees had been the best friend at school of Olivia Shakespear's daughter, Dorothy. Born in 1892, Bertha, known as 'Georgie', was introduced to Yeats in 1910 and began to assist in the collation of his notes on supernatural communication. When Iseult Gonne refused his proposal, Yeats declared to Lady Gregory his intention of marrying Georgie. He proposed and was accepted. In October 1917, the 52-year-old Yeats and the 26-year-old Georgie were married in a civil ceremony at a north London registry office. They were to have two children, Anne in 1919 and Michael in 1921. The settlement of marriage and family life, along with a reawakening of psychic and imaginative energy which can be attributed to Georgie, led to the last, and greatest, period of Yeats's work.

A VISION

Georgie shared an interest in the occult with her husband and, after they were married, she took up automatic writing, feeling her hand, as it held a pencil over paper, moved by an external force as if something were using her as a medium to write. Yeats was tremendously excited by this and experimentation led to what he termed a new framework and patterns. This new insight into history and historical patterns gained from the spirit messages, led to the writing of A Vision. This expounding of a personal philosophical system gave Yeats's poetry a new life and energy, a new system of metaphors, images and symbols which

---

KEY FACT

Partition and the Civil War
The Easter Rising renewed nationalist zeal amongst the Irish population and Sinn Fein was elected to represent an increased majority in 1918. The political party refused to go to Westminster, however, and set up an illegal parliament in Dublin. This led to a war for independence with the British and the presence in Ireland of the Black and Tans, an auxiliary force whose brutal behaviour made the British hated even more. In 1922, the Anglo-Irish Treaty led to partition, the division of Ireland into the 26 counties of the South, the Irish Free State, and the six counties of Ulster in the North, still giving allegiance to the British crown. This was seen as a sell-out by many and led to a bloody, year-long civil war between those who wanted a united Ireland entirely independent of the British and those who thought partition an acceptable compromise.

tempered the disillusionment of the poems of the middle period. Instead, the beauty of the early poems was united with the strength of those of the middle period to form his remarkable mature work.

SUCCESS – A PUBLIC MAN

Yeats had bought a Norman Castle, Thoor Ballylee, in 1915 and, in this last phase of his life, sought to turn it into a symbol, to invest it with deeper significances. The tower became central to his thought and it was from the tower that, at times, he observed – or, at least heard – the strife that was raging through Ireland.

By now, Yeats was a celebrated man. He was awarded the Nobel Prize for Literature in 1923 and became a respected senator of the Irish Free State, formed after the Civil War. It is a mark of the esteem in which he was held that, when Yeats died in 1939, it was suggested that his body be interred in St Patrick's Cathedral, Dublin.

DEATH

Throughout the 1920s and 1930s, Yeats's health gave cause for concern; from high blood pressure to an attack of Maltese fever in 1929, the symptoms of which were so severe that Yeats thought he was going to die and he drew up his will. His career in the Senate was cut short by a series of illnesses – arthritis, flu and even measles. In 1935, Yeats suffered congestion of the lung and, in 1936, kidney problems. He had taken to spending winters in southern Europe for the climate. The last days of Yeats's life, in 1939, were spent with family and friends on the Côte D'Azur. He was in good spirits, looked well and was writing. However, he declined suddenly, falling into a coma in which he died on 28 January. Yeats was buried in France but, in 1948, his remains were exhumed and finally laid to rest in Sligo. By the time he died, Yeats had finished the corrections to and revisions of his last poems, having determined the order in which his latest volume of collected poems was to be set.

CHRONOLOGY OF SELECTED MAJOR WORKS

It must be remembered that Yeats's work was in a constant state of revision, rewriting and re-editing. Some of the dates below refer to the date of publication, some to the date of writing and, some to the appearance of a collection of poetry in its final form rather than in its original.

1889 *The Wanderings of Oisin* (narrative poem)
      Crossways (lyric poetry)
1891 *John Sherman*
      Dhoya (prose fiction)
1892 *The Countess Cathleen* (play)
1897 *William Blake and the Imagination* (essay)
1898 *Symbolism in Painting* (essay)
1893 *The Celtic Twilight* (folk tales)
      The Rose (lyric poetry)
1894 *The Land of Heart's Desire* (play)
1897 *The Celtic Element in Literature* (essay)
      The Secret Rose
      Tables of the Law
      Adoration of the Magi (fiction)
1899 *The Wind Among the Reeds* (lyric poetry)
1900 *The Symbolism of Poetry* (essay)
1901 *Magic* (essay)
1903 *Pot O' Broth* (play)
1904 *In the Seven Woods* (lyric poetry)
1905 *Stories of Red Hanrahan* (fiction)
1906 *The Shadowy Waters* (play)
1907 *Deirdre* (play)
1910 *The Green Helmet* (lyric poetry)
1914 *Responsibilities* (lyric poetry)
1915 *Reveries over Childhood and Youth* (autobiographical writing)
1917 *Per Amica Silentia Lunae* (occult writing)
      At the Hawk's Well (play)

1919 *The Wild Swans at Coole* (lyric poetry)
1921 *Michael Robartes and the Dancer* (lyric poetry)
1922 *Trembling of the Veil* (autobiographical prose)
          The Player Queen (play)
1925 *A Vision* (occult writing)
1926 *The Cat and the Moon* (play)
1928 *The Tower*
1933 *The Winding Stair*
          Other Poems (lyric poetry)
1935 *A Full Moon in March* (play)
1937 *A Vision* (revised)
          A General Introduction for my Work (essay)
1938 *New Poems* (lyric poetry)
          The Herne's Egg (play)
1939 *Last Poems* (lyric poetry)
          On the Boiler (essays)
          The Death of Cuchulain (play)

Many of the essays and fictions were gathered together in collections such as *Mythologies* (1934) and *Autobiographies* (first published 1955), sometimes with changes made from the original. The order of stories in *The Secret Rose* as they appear in *Mythologies*, for example, is very different from the order published in 1897. More details will be given in the Further Reading section.

❋ ❋ ❋ *SUMMARY* ❋ ❋ ❋

- Yeats's writing adds up to a unification of his life and times.

- Yeats was a respected poet and important public man in his lifetime.

- We can divide Yeats's work into three periods.

- Although the poems lie at the centre of any study of Yeats, you should also consider his other work – fiction, plays and essays.

Major Themes

4

There are ideas and concerns, images and symbols which recur throughout Yeats's writing. Themes raised in his early work are still present in the later work, developed and explored or revisited from the changing perspectives of age and experience.

CREATING UNITY

Yeats wanted his work to express, as far as possible, the complete experience of a man throughout his life; shaped and worked by art into a permanent form available to whomever would read it then and in future generations. He was writing for a public and for posterity, representing his life as a work of art, one indistinguishable from the other. He wanted his work to be seen as a **canon**; each poem, essay, story, even letter contributing to it and forming a representation of himself and his times. Consequently, at various times during his life, he re-edited his work, frequently updating and reorganizing, even requesting that letters he had sent be returned to him for revision before publication.

> **KEYWORD**
>
> Canon: the recognized genuine works of any author.

At the time of his death, Yeats was busy revising the order in which his last poems would appear in a collected edition. What we now read, therefore, is a deliberately refined and shaped collection of writing which adds up to as complete a representation of a life as is possible. Yeats made the incidents of his life, his family, his remarkable circle of friends, his feelings, his thoughts and his surroundings the subjects of his work, in many ways recreating himself through his poems, in his dealings with others and in his relationship to the political, cultural, religious and historical world in which he lived. The idea that life and work should stand separately would not have found sympathy with Yeats: for him, the life is the art and the art is the life. In an epilogue to the 1908 revised collected edition of his work, Yeats answered critics who had complained about his constant revision of his work:

> *The friends that have I do it wrong*
> *Whenever I remake a song*
> *Should know what issue is at stake –*
> *It is myself that I remake.*

AUTOBIOGRAPHY

The body of Yeats's work may be read, therefore, as an autobiography, but not as memoirs. In memoirs, the external details of a life are described chronologically through anecdote, with some reflection upon the effect of events upon the protagonist and possibly some reworking to present the subject in a better light, or with an eye to the libel laws. However honest the conventional autobiographer may be, there is still the sense of a life viewed from the perspective of distance, a looking back. This is not the case with Yeats who shaped and crafted his words to reveal the passion of immediacy. The purpose of all this revision was to get as close as possible to reality. He wrote in a letter to Lady Elizabeth Pelham: 'Man can embody the truth, but he cannot know it.' He believed that the universe was coherent, that it made sense and had purpose and that truth and coherence could be shown through the close examination of a life and all that pertained to it. The significance of the circumstances of a life could be seen in cosmic, rather than merely local, terms. Like any autobiographical writer, Yeats writes of his family and friends, but his aims and methods are radically different.

MYTHOLOGIES

Part of the process is to mythologize, to link the here and now with the universal by seeing it in terms of **archetypes**.

> **KEYWORD**
>
> Archetypes: literally, an original model, a proto-type. The psychologist Carl Jung used the term to mean primordial images which exist in the collective unconscious and appear throughout history in various myth-ical forms or motifs.

Thus, George Pollexfen, Yeats's uncle who was an astrologer and with whom Yeats conducted experiments in second sight, became invested with the mantle of seer and mystic, linked through this designation with the seers and mystics of the past. Lady Gregory and her home at Coole Park, while in one sense fixed in time and place, in another sense became representations of a certain sort of aristocratic grandeur tempered by courtesy and modesty, the symbol of a continuity of ideas, codes of behaviour and the history of a culture.

Maud Gonne is linked to such mythical figures as Helen of Troy, offspring of Leda and Zeus, who disguised himself as a swan to seduce Leda. At various times, Maud Gonne is represented as a symbol of unrequited love, of passionate beauty diverted into ignoble and violent causes, of lost beauty and tragic grandeur. It is not so much that Yeats, like Blake, created a mythology, but that he wove the actual and transient into a cosmic and historical fabric which endows them with significance so that they become 'beautiful lofty things' and 'all the Olympians' ('Beautiful Lofty Things').

MASKS

And what of the poet himself? Yeats wanted to find truth and reality but, as he implied in his letter to Lady Pelham, he could not know it – at least, not as long as he was hemmed in, constrained by the limitations of personality and personal history. A moment's reflection will show us that the 'I' of which we talk so freely is a complex and multi-faceted thing, bewildering in its diversity: we can discern many contradictory aspects of our personalities. There is also the question of the versions of 'I' which we choose to present to other people. In 'The Love Song of J. Alfred Prufrock', T.S. Eliot wrote that there is time in life to 'prepare a face to meet the faces that we meet' – to assume appropriate social roles suitable for different occasions, to come up with variations upon the theme of 'I', versions of ourselves. How do we determine, how can we know, our true selves? Yeats's answer to this was, in part, that reality does not lie in any one aspect of ourselves or in any one facet of our personalities or characters, but in the

interaction between them. Yeats was, apparently, unaware of the work of the psychologist Jung, but the theory which he developed and called 'the doctrine of the mask' bears strong resemblance to some of Jung's theories about the relationship between the conscious and unconscious minds. Reality lies in the tension between the hidden self, whose influences and impulses rule our lives, and the conscious mask, what Yeats called the 'anti-self', which we adopt to express ourselves.

Part of the discipline of the artist is to be aware of these tensions, to be in control, to understand how the masks can be adopted, to present the face which is needed. When Yeats was in London in his early twenties, he was by most accounts, including his own, shy, self-conscious, unhappy and, in the words of Richard Ellman, 'painfully aware of the vast gulf between what he was in actuality and what he was in his dreams' (Yeats: *The Man and the Masks*, Penguin, 1987, p.78).

Yeats's meeting with Maud Gonne in 1889 and his immediate response to her seemed to bring these issues to a head, polarizing the types of dreamer and man of action. The poetry of this period is dreamy, wistful, full of unrequited passion and longing. The image projected is of one who loves passionately, but in vain. Maud Gonne, however, could not be dealt with in these terms: she was a fiery, passionate woman actively involved in revolutionary politics and drawn to men of action.

In the years following their first meeting and Yeats's emergence as something of a public figure himself, at least outwardly demonstrating poise and confidence, comes the creation of two characters, Michael Robartes and Owen Aherne. They were to play a continuing part in Yeats's representation of his inner struggle and his attempts to reconcile the masks necessary to face the world with the self. Yeats externalized these dualities again and again in his poetry, his plays and his stories. He came to believe that each man could recreate himself, form his own character, present himself as the opposite of what he knows himself to be and seek union with his opposite. The doctrine of the mask becomes, therefore, not just a way of assuming appropriate fronts when necessary, but a way of drawing up all possibilities into one experience and personality, gaining control of the self, and through the self, of the outside world. Later, in *A Vision*, this philosophy was systematized in a pattern of astrological complexity. Here, types of human personality were allocated to phases of the moon within a cycle, through which the individual soul would pass during the course of a lifetime, or across the course of several. Each phase has its opposite, its mask.

In 'Among Schoolchildren', written when Yeats was an important public figure, the outward appearance of the 'sixty year old smiling man' being shown around school by 'a kind old nun in a white hood' is a mask for the passionate interior, stirred by memories and speculations evoked by the children around him.

The mask, of course, has links to the theatre, since actors adopt different characters and find the means to portray emotions, ideas and experiences which may be very different from their own. It is also part of the process of mythologizing: the images and the faces presented by the masks adopted resonate through history as types personified in every age and every mythology, and are another way of establishing a relationship with powerful spiritual forces.

MAGIC

By magic, Yeats meant all the hidden and secret matters known as the occult, and he declared that, next to poetry, the study of magic was the most important pursuit of his life. He believed that there was a reality outside the grasp of the five senses and beyond the reach of the dull empiricism of Science and that there were real correspondences between the world of the spirit and the material world. The unities which he wanted to find, of life, of self, of art, of history, could not exist unless there was an ordered, cohesive universe. Throughout his life, he was involved with the occult as a member of organizations such as the Theosophical Society and the Hermetic Students of the Golden Dawn. These taught that, by studying books of esoteric wisdom, by the practice of ritual and through incantation and practical magic, the individual soul could attain knowledge of the secret patterns of the universe. Yeats studied books of secret wisdom drawn from a variety of religious and mystical backgrounds. He studied books of Oriental and Eastern systems, the Jewish Kabbala, the Greek and Roman mystery religions, Christian mysticism and apocrypha.

The reality contained within could only be known and expressed through symbol, and Yeats took from each system what he needed for his own emerging system of symbols and images, using and developing them in his poetry. Later in his life, Yeats took a great interest in spiritualism, attending seances and communing with the dead, contacting a spirit guide named Leo Africanus.

After his marriage and the discovery of his wife's automatic writing, Yeats worked on *A Vision* in which he explained the whole system of correspondences, patterns and cycles which would inform the magnificent late period of his work. It is a fusion of various sources, of images and symbols drawn from many areas into an original pattern. It is deterministic, showing patterns of the past and future and, indeed, Yeats used it for prophetic purposes. The need to classify, to systematize and, through systemization, to control, is clear. Here, Yeats gathered up all that had gone before and found new unity and purpose. His **symbolist** background, his use of symbols to express the

> **KEYWORD**
>
> Symbolist: a late nine-teenth-century movement in art and poetry which saw the actual world as a representation or ex-pression of something else.

otherwise inexpressible, his use of archetypes and myths to make universal, now seem resolved into one huge symbol.

THE IMPORTANCE OF SYMBOLISM

All figurative language serves the same purpose: to express ideas, emotions or states of being for which ordinary language is inadequate. Thus, if we were in a hurry to get home, for example, we might say, 'I tore down the road'. The metaphorical use of the word 'tore' suggests more speed and urgency than is contained in the literal verb 'ran'. Symbolism works in the same way. In Tennyson's 'In Memoriam', the poet describes himself as 'an infant crying in the night, and with no language but a cry'. The infant and the cry represent, or symbolize, the poet's feeling of ignorance and helplessness in the face of the enormity of death. Because we can all make the association between the helpless infant and Tennyson's feeling of impotence, the symbol is effective and conveys exactly what the poet intended. In *The Merchant of Venice*, a candle shining in the dark night symbolizes 'a good deed in a naughty world', and, again the association is clear. We can all think of good examples from our favourite works of literature.

One of the pleasures of reading a poet's complete works, written over a lifetime, is that one can see how the poet has chosen symbols peculiar to his or her own concerns and how they have been explored and developed in a variety of contexts during a period of time. Yeats's poetry is particularly rich in symbolism, much of it being drawn from his occult readings and from sources such as the tarot pack, as well as from more personal sources. You will note the frequent appearance of the sun, the moon, trees, birds, towers, roses and masks, among other images, which recur and you will see how they are used to convey meaning.

Increasingly in Yeats's poetry, however, a symbol is not simply one way of conveying a particular meaning or mood. The early influence of the symbolist movement was strong, a movement which believed in the power of symbolism to find a reality which cannot be caught by other means. The relationship between the symbol and the symbolized is complex. For Yeats, a poem does not simply contain symbolism, it is a symbol in itself. A finished poem stands for a mood and, because the arrangement of its elements is worked, refined, made as perfect as it can be, that mood cannot be expressed in another way. Since, as we have seen, Yeats saw his work as a complete unit, it is fair to say that his whole canon is a symbol of his life, and indistinguishable from his life: 'who can tell the dancer from the dance?' ('Among Schoolchildren'). This view was consolidated following *A Vision*, after which he consciously arranged his life and all in it as a symbolic whole, investing his home, its furnishings, his garden, all around him, with deeper significance, as here in the 1928 poem, 'Blood and the Moon', he wrote:

I declare this tower is my symbol; I declare
This winding, gyring, spiring treadmill of a stair is my ancestral stair.

The search for unity, 'to fuse life, work, country into one indissoluble whole', the 'lifelong effort to cast all experience into symbol' is the abiding theme of Yeats's writing (Richard Ellman, *Yeats: The Man and the Masks*, Penguin, 1987).

IRELAND

Although Yeats spent some of his early years in England and although, throughout his life, he was frequently away from Ireland, his love for his country and his aspirations for it – even when exasperated with it – are clear. Much of the early poetry, his plays and his prose are concerned with the creation of a cultural identity which he felt was ignored by those who, it seemed to him, looked no further than mere political independence. Yeats heard the folk tales of the people in Sligo where, as a child, he would go with his mother on breaks from London life and he published them in 1888 as *Fairy and Folk Tales*. One year later appeared 'The Wanderings of Oisin', a narrative poem with its roots in Irish legend, but provided with a symbolic framework that also contains aspects of personal and national experience.

Already, the link is made between Ireland and Yeats. This use of Irish legend as a means of identifying self with history and myth continues through the early poems with their dreamy, Pre-Raphaelite imagery and cadences. By the early 1890s, Yeats's stated intention was to stimulate interest in Irish things and he worked to bring about an Irish literary renaissance, establishing literary societies, writing and promoting plays on Irish themes to be presented in the Irish theatre that he founded.

The poems and the plays lean heavily upon the mystical and heroic – stories of Cuchulain, Fergus, Deirdre, the Sidhe and the Wandering Aengus. Many of these figures become part of the many aspects of Yeats's character, his masks, a means of exploration. In a series of poems in which the poet is represented as 'he' or 'Aedh', the cloths of heaven are wished for, past greatness is recalled and forgotten beauty is remembered. In prose in *The Celtic Twilight*, the poet, in the style of a folklorist travelling around the west of Ireland and hearing folk tales, recounts stories and legends of the supernatural. In poems and prose, Irish legends are put into juxtaposition with images from Christianity and from classical mythology to form a magical world in which Christianity and paganism interweave. The aim is to create for Ireland a culture based on its mythology, a heroic culture, imaginative, spiritual and linked with other great spiritual and imaginative cultures.

This was how Yeats hoped to bring Ireland out of the doldrums into which the death of Parnell and the apparent end to any sight of Home Rule had cast it. This was the view which Yeats had of the spirit that would infuse an independent Ireland, an independence beyond the merely political. Others, however, required a more immediate and practical end and were prepared to use force to achieve it. It is to be expected that Yeats, with his desire for unity, would fear and detest factions. Although he joined organizations which had on their agendas the immediate expulsion of the British from Ireland, he felt that politics, by and large, was a sordid business and he was appalled by the violence expressed and the in-fighting which seem to be endemic to any revolutionary movement. He was more concerned with Ireland as a whole, with its spiritual and intellectual life rather than just – as he would have seen it – her political future. Speeches made in London and New York around the turn of the century show him wanting an Ireland in which 'not only will the wealth be well distributed, but there will be an imaginative culture and power to understand imaginative and spiritual things distributed among the people' (quoted in Richard Ellman, *Yeats: The Man and the Masks*, Penguin, 1987). Here is the desire, not just to liberate Ireland politically, but to improve it culturally and spiritually.

Yeats's relationships with Maud Gonne and Lady Gregory are important here. Lady Gregory shared his vision of Ireland's future, helping him with his Irish writings and the founding of the theatre, writing plays and stories and providing a haven of calm for him when he needed one. This calm, patrician atmosphere can be contrasted with the fraught relationship with Maud Gonne and her desire for action. His attitude towards the rebels and particularly John MacBride is, at times, scathing, and he represents them at first as narrow and petty, lacking in vision. Yeats's exasperation with Ireland, his sadness at the failure of people to see what he was trying to do and their reception to some of the plays put on at the Abbey can be seen in the poetry of the middle period when he turns away from the old stories and imagery, and the tone of the poems become sharper, more attuned to the rhythms and diction of speech than the Romantic style of apostrophe and declamation. At the same time, Yeats stopped writing plays for a while and a new bitterness and sense of loss pervades the poems. Although what he saw of revolutionary republicanism appalled him, he recognized the heroism of the men who took part in the Easter rebellion and made it a part of his own system. Through events, through action rather than through introspection, ordinary men, including the 'drunken vainglorious lout' ('Easter 1916') MacBride, had found their masks, their opposites, and been transformed into heroes.

The vision for Ireland expounded in Yeats's speeches in New York and London show that Yeats was not a democrat but, however benignly, he was autocratic and authoritarian, and these tendencies increase throughout the poems. During the civil war of 1922, when Yeats could hear the sound of fighting from his tower at Thoor Ballylee, his anxiety for his country was great, and his conservatism takes new and potentially dangerous paths. His love of order and unity is applied to political order, always implicit in his respect for the aristocracy and his wish to associate himself with them in various ways. His vision of an Ireland in which all know their place in a fixed social scheme, which mirrors a cosmic scheme, led Yeats into brief sympathy for the fascist parties arising in Europe and particularly in Mussolini's Italy. For a while, in the 1930s, Yeats was intrigued by an Irish Fascist party called the Blue Shirts, but the attraction was short-lived.

In later poetry, when life, art and symbol fused, Yeats declared that the Irish Renaissance had taken place in the seventeenth century, the time of Swift and Berkely, and he believed that, as the cycles of time turned, another was coming.

HISTORY AND PROPHECY

Yeats developed views about history and destiny which were based on the systems expounded in *A Vision* and were illustrated by one of the most important later symbols – the gyres. Picture the gyres as two cones which penetrate each other, the nose of each against the base of the other. These cones, or gyres, represent the opposites in the nature of each person or country or historical period. As the diagram

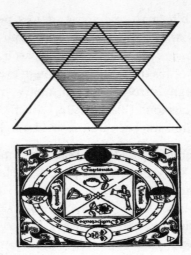

illustrating the gyres indicates, each entity contains elements of both opposites, categorized as lunar and solar, or subjective and objective, or moral and aesthetic. One gyre is the primary gyre, the other the antithetical gyre and, through space and time, one or the other becomes dominant. Hence, in 'The Second Coming' the gyre of the Christian era is coming to an end to be succeeded by its antithesis:

> *And what rough beast, its hour come round at last,*
> *Slouches towards Bethlehem to be born?*

By this system, the past can be classified and the future predicted. In *A Vision*, the doctrine of the mask is also thoroughly systematized in another symbol – the Great Wheel. The Great Wheel has 28 spokes, representing a year set out in lunar months. Each spoke represents the 28 possible selves, each being a mask of the one opposite, the 28 phases of each person's life and the phases of each cycle of world history, each cycle being approximately 2,000 years long – reference again to the coming end of 2,000 years of Christianity in 'The Second Coming'. Systems are important throughout the poems, but the systems of *A Vision* inform all the later poetry.

LOVE

The development of Yeats's feelings and thoughts about love may be traced through the poems. The early poems, wistful, longing, often dealing with unrequited love and demonstrating the feelings of the dreaming artist as opposed to the man of action, give way to a disappointment and a bitterness in the middle period. Youthful idealism gives way to experience.

It is love for Maud Gonne which brings to the fore the location and polarization of self and mask via Robartes and Aherne; and it is her rejection of Yeats in favour of MacBride that takes Yeats into the second phase of his writing. Here, he loses the air of sentimental introspection and the romantic flavour of the verse, which becomes more forceful and direct, allowing the rhythms and idioms of speech. In the last, magnificently productive, period, Yeats returns to the theme of love, writing again of Maud Gonne and his passion for her. Now, however, he is remembering passion and his expression is tempered by an emotion which, although strong, is more analytical and reflective.

DEATH AND OLD AGE

Yeats's feelings about old age and death are treated in various ways throughout the poems, from the wisdom and spirituality of the hermits and beggars of his early verse to the anger in his later verse at the fact that this wisdom is bought at the price of physical infirmity and impending death. Yeats returns again and again, also, to the nature of poetry and the means of producing it, the difficulty of finding words and the time taken to find the right order for them.

❋ ❋ ❋*SUMMARY*❋ ❋ ❋

- Many of the themes of Yeats's work are explored across the course of his lifetime.

- Yeats's life is his work and vice versa: the artist and the art are indivisible.

- Reality lies in the interaction of self and anti-self, and it is the business of the individual, particularly the artist, to strive to find and become his or her opposite.

- Much of Yeats's systems and imagery are drawn from occult studies, synthesizing principles and symbols.

- Everything is symbol.

- Everything and everyone passes through cycles or phases of existence during the course of space and time.

Major Works 5

It is recommended that Yeats's work should be read, as far as possible, in the order in which it has come to us. This brief guide to the major works will, therefore, present the material chronologically, rather than in separate sections for poems, drama and prose. Yeats rewrote and reorganized his work throughout his life to present a cohesive picture of the development of his ideas and art. This means that there are differences between each edition of the collected works, depending upon when they were compiled.

Not all readers will have access to a university library and so references are confined to the two volumes of collected poetry which are most readily available in public libraries or in high street bookshops. They are the 1933 *Collected Poems* published by Macmillan, and the *Everyman* edition first published in 1990. The 1933 edition collects narrative verse at the back of the book, with lyrical poetry at the front. The *Everyman* edition presents them in chronological order.

1888–1904

'The Wanderings of Oisin' and *John Sherman*

Yeats wanted the poem 'The Wanderings of Oisin' (pronounced Usheen) from its place among the narrative poems, to precede the first book of lyrical poems *Crossways*, thus indicating that this is where he wanted his readers to start. It is a poem which deals with Irish matter rather than the Arcadian and Indian pieces which begin the lyrics. 'Oisin' was written in 1888 and published in 1899, winning good reviews from, among others, Oscar Wilde. It is an Irish legend reworked to carry some of the themes and symbols which Yeats would develop over the years. The abhorrence of old age and the anger that wisdom is only attained at the cost of approaching death and declining faculties is there, as is the love of antithesis, the ways in which opposites and dualities are identified. Images are used to carry discrete meanings and are also woven into symbolic themes. Yeats said, 'The whole poem is full of symbols', particularly in the second half where, 'I have said several things to which only I have the key' (Letter to Katherine Tynan, quoted in Richard Ellman, *Yeats: The Man and the Mask*, Penguin, 1979).

The presence of birds – coloured birds, Asian birds, ravens, eagles, parrots which rejuvenate themselves – is, perhaps, the most obvious use of symbols which run throughout Yeats's work.

The use of autobiography is raised here also and will be discussed in Chapter 7. It is raised in relation to two short works of fiction, *John Sherman*, completed in 1885 but first published in 1891 with *Dhoya*. Both stories were included in the 1908 edition of Yeats's *Collected Works* with a preface stating that 'they have come to interest me deeply'.

(preface to *John Sherman* (1907) reprinted in *Short Fiction*, G.J.Watson, Penguin, 1995).

Whereas 'Oisin' is the story of its mythical hero's journeys to three islands during the course of 300 years, before his return to Ireland, *John Sherman* is about a man who leaves his home in Ballah, west Ireland, to work in his uncle's firm in London, marrying Margaret Leland before realizing that he belongs in Ballah with Mary Carton. 'Oisin' is told in verse with a variety of metres and rhyme schemes with heroic, romantic diction, while the style of the short story gives the impression of a story being told rather than written, despite some highly descriptive passages and one or two **Wildean** epigrams.

> **KEYWORD**
>
> Wildean: In the manner of Oscar Wilde, nineteenth-century wit and dramatist, famous for his prolific output of memorable sayings, quips and put-downs.

Opposites and the Centre of Unity

Both pieces establish the pattern of opposites. John Sherman, the reflective dreamer, is cast against William Howard, man of action and his great friend, despite their friendship being founded in 'a great measure of mutual contempt'. The peaceful country setting of Ballah is contrasted with the barrenness of London, with images of the fecundity of one put into juxtaposition with the single pear tree growing in a London front garden in the other. The simplicity and naturalness of Mary Carton is contrasted with the sophistication of Margaret, an atheist who wears a silver cross for adornment, and whose bright eyes, which so attract John Sherman, are achieved by the application of belladonna. Whereas in 'Oisin', Yeats seemed not to want us to recognize the symbols, in *John Sherman*, they are pointed out to us by the author. The three symbols of Sherman's life, for example, and the family on the train which takes him back to London who become 'ominous symbols', their 'smooth faces shining with well-being'.

In *Dhoya*, we see the interaction of the natural and supernatural world, so common in folk tales which will become important in Yeats' poetry. The importance of Irish legend and folklore is present, explicitly or implicitly, in all three works and in the return to Ireland of both Oisin and John Sherman, we can see each character finding his 'centre of unity' and obeying the law of his being.

Crossways and The Rose

Crossways (1899) and The Rose (1893) are the first two volumes of lyric poetry in the Collected Poems, but neither appeared originally in this form. The poems which form Crossways represent a selection of the ways tried by Yeats to present his subjects, while the poems gathered in The Rose represent the path towards beauty and peace which he finally chose, symbolized by the eternal rose. Yeats edited both into clear and cohesive order. In Crossways, eight poems are set in Arcady or India, while eight deal with Irish subjects, reflecting the range of Yeats's search for the right path. The poems are linked by ideas. 'The Happy Shepherd', for example, lives in a grey modern world where 'the woods of Arcady are dead', as are, 'the kings of the old time', but he believes that his power to use words can revive poetic imagination. The sad shepherd, however, lacks the power to act. As always, there are linking ideas and images – music, the sea-shell – and the idea that truth will not be found by scientists and astronomers, the 'starry men' who lack poetic imagination and to which, unfortunately, the modern age is drawn. Reality, the collection reminds us, lies in the perception of the individual.

The rose is the symbol of perfection and spiritual beauty, a common enough use in Christian mysticism, its eastern equivalent being the lotus. Yeats makes the symbol fluid, however. It can represent a golden age of Irish spirituality, untainted by materialism. It can stand for the beauty and perfection of a woman, such as Maud Gonne, and also the end of the world, an apocalypse. The poem 'The Rose Upon the Rood of Time', with its image of the rose crucified, suggests that this symbol of perfection, Christ-like, understands and shares the anguish of those who seek it, while in 'The Secret Rose', which prefaces a collection of stories first appearing in 1897 and appears in the 1899 collection The Wind Among the Reeds, it is 'far off, most secret and inviolate', more distant and unapproachable.

The collection of stories, *The Secret Rose*, again is carefully arranged in a particular order. The theme is the war between the natural and the spiritual order, and the stories explore this theme across centuries of Irish history. One story is set in pre-Christian time, two in the monastic age, three in the seventeenth century and the final three in what, to Yeats, was modern Ireland. They are all set in the west of Ireland and, in the last three, Michael Robartes and Owen Aherne, those representations of different aspects of their creator, appear. Still more aspects of Yeats appear in the collection of poems *The Wind Among the Reeds*, and a dominant image is of shape-shifting and elusiveness. There are fish, slippery and silvery, eluding capture in the water and, in 'The Rose', the image of Maud Gonne 'that blossoms a rose in the deeps of my heart.'

Seven Woods

By the time of *In the Seven Woods* (1904) Maud Gonne had married and Yeats was concentrating more on the theatre than on lyric poetry. The seven woods were the woods of Lady Gregory's Coole Park estate. In this collection, changes are taking place. The supernatural and 'faery' world is still important, but the natural world is coming more to the fore, reflected in a diction and in cadences more attuned to speech than the heroic tone of much of the previous work. Two poems were added to this collection in time for the 1908 *Collected Works*. Both advise the lover not to love too much or for too long, since, as Yeats admits in 'O Do Not Love Too Long':

> *I loved long and long*
> *And grew to be out of fashion*
> *Like an old song.*

1904–1917

The public man, plays and *The Green Helmet*

In the years between *In the Seven Woods* and *The Green Helmet* (1911), Yeats became a successful public man. He wrote few lyrics, but concentrated upon his work with his theatre, as well as undertaking lecture tours in America and putting together the 1908 edition of his collected works.

The plays, true to Yeats's idea of the theatre's purposes, had been serious explorations of Irish stories and themes, such as the nature of heroic sacrifice in *Cathleen Ni Houlihan* (1902), set at the time of the uprising in 1798, in which Michael Gillane leaves his private world to join the patriots, or in *The King's Threshold* (1904) which explores one of Yeats's recurring themes, the relationship between the man of dreams and the man of action. In *The Green Helmet,* the poems presented are, as usual, ordered carefully. The first eight poems take Maud Gonne as their subject, exploring Yeats's feelings for her and her responses. 'Reconciliations' records his reactions when he heard of her marriage, while in other poems she becomes mythical, aligned with Helen of Troy, a woman Homer sung. In 'All Things Can Tempt Me', Yeats reflects upon the irony that the matters which distracted him from writing when young have now become the subject matter of his writing.

Other poems see Yeats in public places, such as the theatre or the races, more confident and at ease than the love-lorn poet and dreamer of previous books. The style of the poems, with their more conversational cadences, reflect the changes in attitude, perhaps echoed in the intention to 'hurl helmets, crowns and swords into the pit'. The time was coming also when Yeats would temporarily lose his enthusiasm for the Irish stage. This was brought on, in part, by the responses of the audiences to the plays. It is instructive here to pause and read his play *Deirdre* which was first performed in 1906, and *The Shadowy Waters*, one of his most revised pieces, first produced in 1904. This latter play came, apparently from visionary experiences, and is even farther removed from conventional theatre than Yeats's other plays, being highly stylized and ritualized. After having seen it in production, Yeats proposed making revisions which would involve thinning out the number of symbols in the play and making the characters answer each other. *Deirdre* is based on a story from Celtic myth, so its subject matter would have been familiar and Yeats follows it fairly closely. Deirdre is a recognizable character as well as a symbol and vehicle for the play's themes. The language of the play is also different from that of others. Previously, Yeats had delineated heroic and peasant characters in the dialogue, the heroes speaking heroic verse, the peasants speaking dialect, something which gave him considerable trouble in writing. In 'Deirde', the language is more unified and, like that of the poems, more attuned to the rhythms of speech.

Still, audiences were critical, both of the high-flown verse–drama and of realistic works which offended their sensibilities, culminating in the violent scenes at the opening of Synge's *Playboy of the Western World*. Bearing this in mind, maybe the change in Yeats's tone is most obviously caught in 'At the Abbey Theatre', when the man whose lofty ambitions for a spiritual Ireland reflected in Irish theatre complains:

> *When we are high and airy hundreds say*
> *That if we hold that flight they'll lave the place,*
> *While those same hundreds mock another day*
> *Because we have made our art of common things.*

Also in this collection comes the first poem explicitly on the subject of the mask, in which a woman who asks for her companion's mask to be removed is told that it is the mask that holds her, and it does not matter what is beneath it: the artifice has become the reality. Other poems take Coole Park as their subject and Yeats's growing fear that the estate, what it represents and, by extension, the qualities it gives to Ireland, might be threatened by sordid commerce and the cost of upkeep. Here also is the idea of an aristocracy which offers right government, ideas and art to the masses.

Responsibilities

The collection *Responsibilities*, which appeared in 1914, is, as it appears in its place in the collected poems, a summing up, an evaluation of Yeats's concerns and subject matters thus far. In the introductory poem, Yeats tells his ancestors:

> *I have no child and nothing but a book*
> *Nothing but that to prove your blood and mine.*

This is a statement of responsibility to his forefathers, almost a promise that in his writing he will keep faith with them. Among other responsibilities acknowledged in this collection are the responsibilities befitting a public man. He comments upon topical matters, among them the riots at the Abbey Theatre and the failure of the authorities to take advantage of Lady Gregory's nephew's offer to donate his collection of paintings to the Dublin Gallery of Modern Art. This develops a theme always implicit, but stated ever more clearly: Yeats's disgust at the rise of the commercial and bourgeois. The autocratic and patrician tone noted before is here again. 'Romantic Ireland's dead and gone', we are told, killed, presumably, by those who 'fumble in a greasy till/And add the halfpence to the pence' ('September 1913').

The view that a subscription to the gallery would be made only if 'it were proved that the People wanted pictures' is met with the response that the Duke D'Ercol, a medieval patron of the arts who paid for plays to be staged in an Italian town, did not care 'what th'onion sellers thought or did' ('To a Wealthy Man'). Those who rejected Synge's play are dismissed contemptuously as eunuchs struck dumb by the 'sinewy thigh' of the great lover Don Juan ('On Those That Hated "The Playboy of the Western World"', 1907).

There are statements of responsibility towards Maud and Iseult Gonne, one charactersized as 'fallen majesty', the other as a 'child dancing in the wind', and towards Lady Gregory. The collection closes with 'The Coat', which seems to announce a change, a shift in style and theme to come, in which Yeats will be 'walking naked'. This collection is almost a stocktaking, a discarding of some elements and adoption of others, a response to criticism and an awareness that:

> ...all my priceless things
> Are but a post the passing dogs defile.

It is significant that this was the year in which Yeats began his autobiographies and it would be a good idea to read at this point *Reveries Over Childhood and Youth*, with its recollections of his Sligo relatives, his father and his young self. In 1917, *Per Amica Silentia Lunae* appeared, written at the time of Yeats's seances and exchanges with his spirit guide and which expanded upon his ideas about antitheses, masks and the fate of the soul after death.

Upheavals and the Wild Swans

In the five years between *Responsibilities* and the next collection, *The Wild Swans at Coole*, came massive upheavals. This period saw on the global front the beginning of the First World War and, on the national, the Easter Rising. John MacBride was executed; Yeats proposed to Maud Gonne and was rejected for the last time. Iseult Gonne also rejected him. Lady Gregory's son Robert, a pilot, was shot down over Italy and killed. Yeats married Georgie Hyde-Lees, and the revelations that were to lead to *A Vision* began. He bought the tower at Ballylee and prepared to move in.

1919–1939

The Wild Swans at Coole continues some of the work of *Responsibilities*, offering advice to Iseult Gonne, continuing to celebrate Maud Gonne, although recognizing that she is now, like him, middle aged. In a series of poems on the theme of the Mask, Yeats anticipates moving from a lunar, feminine, imaginative phase into a solar, masculine, realistic one, and the opening poems deal movingly with the question of mortality and immortality. The swans which Yeats had looked at on the lake at Coole for the past 19 years function on water and in air, rising from the surface of the lake or drifting on the water, mysterious, beautiful, becoming a metaphor either for immortality or for mortality giving the illusion of immortality.

This poem leads us into a series of poems about the death of Robert Gregory in which he becomes, first a type for all young men of promise who die early, and then a young man who, almost god-like in his 'lonely impulse of delight' ('An Irish Airman Foresees His Death'), lends meaning by his death to an otherwise meaningless conflict. There are also poems about the tower in which Yeats and his family were to live, as he begins the process of turning it into symbol, displaying correspondences between the spiritual and material world, the past and the present. Preparations to occupy the tower lead Yeats to 'name the friends that cannot sup with us' ('In Memory of Major Robert Gregory') once it has been made into a home, while, in an interpolation between two poems about the systems in *A Vision*, he offers a prayer that the tower will become the symbol of unity he desires. The closing poems in this collection concern images and ideas from what was to become *A Vision*, culminating in Michael Robartes's 'double vision', of the first phase in the cycle, the dark of the moon, and then of the fifteenth phase, the full moon, in which a condition of beauty and magnificence prevails. The vision of organic unity is symbolized by the dancer, who unites body and soul, spirit and flesh.

Revolution and the Dancer

The image of the dancer opens Yeats's next collection, *Michael Robartes and the Dancer*, two years later in 1921. This collection presents a picture of a middle-aged, settled man, mature, married with a young family, against a background of change and violence. There is a group of poems in which Yeats seeks to reassure his wife that what disturbs his mind, what makes him 'saturnine', is not memories of other loves or rivals, but a sense of the Ireland to which he wishes to return, but which has changed, become revolutionary, full of bitterness and violence.

At the centre of the collection are five poems explicitly about the Easter rebellion. In 'Easter 1916', Yeats writes of people he had known or seen, of whom he had formed opinions, transformed into something heroic, yet, at the same time, become fixed, intractable in their purposes, represented by the image of a stone in a river around which all else must flow. Yeats has previously noted how adherence to a cause, unquestioning, has proved the undoing of Maud Gonne, and in his 'Prayer for my Daughter', he warns against 'intellectual hatred' and 'opinion'. Thus, there is something of a paradox in the Easter poems: the rebels have become heroes and martyrs by being essentially unchanged in their aims and opinions. Their sacrifice and martyrdom are now being used by the greedy, corrupt or manipulative, those who: 'must to keep their certainty accuse/All that are different of a base intent' ('The Leaders of the Crowd').

Following this comes the image of 'The Second Coming', the time when one age and its principles are giving way to another, and the nightmare imagery of the new age's Messiah shows the horror of what is on its way. 'Prayer for my Daughter'asks how her generation will fare in the chaos to come. In the poem, Yeats watches his child sleeping, innocent, while outside a violent storm, both actual and symbolic of the coming violence and lack of order, rages. The collection finishes with a short poem 'to be carved on a stone at Thoor Ballylee' recording Yeats's existence and his insight, to be there 'when all is ruin once again'.

The Tower and *A Vision*

Between the publication of *Michael Robartes and the Dancer* and *The Tower*, in 1928, the civil war ended, the Irish Free State was declared and Yeats was appointed as a Senator. He received international recognition with the Nobel Prize in 1923. Yeats was not content, however, to be merely a public institution and he continued to wrestle with the issues that disturbed him. Beneath the mask of the 'sixty year old smiling public man' lay still a passionate and questioning mind, one not content with success and venerability, but one bitter about old age and infirmity, wanting to change, to move and affect people.

The first version of *A Vision* appeared in 1925, describing the Great Wheel and the 28 incarnations of the human soul. It explains the workings of the gyres and reinterprets human history in terms of cyclical movements, each opposite to the other yet participating in the other, a system of dominances and correspondences. It deals with the progress of the soul after death. It finishes, as does the collection *The Tower*, with the poem 'All Soul's Night'. The poems in *The Tower* concern in part the public man and in part the seer, wrestling with the problems of occult systems and arcane meanings.

Yeats considered *The Tower* his finest collection but, upon rereading it, was astonished at its bitterness. He looked forward, he said, to redressing this tone and did so in the next collection, *The Winding Stair*, the title being a reference to the staircase in Thoor Ballylee, a symbol of ascent and positivity.

In *The Tower*, 'Sailing to Byzantium' states that modern Ireland is no place for old men, being violent and troubled. Yeats's ideal is Byzantium, where:

> *maybe never before or since in recorded history*
> *religious, aesthetic and practical life were one.*

The idea that an old man is a 'tattered coat upon a stick', disregarded, expected not to feel passion or physical desire, is taken up again in the opening lines of 'The Tower':

> *Never had I more*
> *Excited, passionate, fanatical*
> *Imagination, nor an ear and eye*
> *That more expected the impossible.*

This theme is continued most movingly in 'Among Schoolchildren', where the public figure, doing what is expected of him, feels emotion stir inside him as the children stir memories:

> *Better to smile on all that smile, and show*
> *There is a comfortable kind of old scarecrow.*

In *The Tower* collection and from now on there is also a remarkable degree of self-knowledge, memories of youthful passions, acts, failures which are held up to scrutiny in poem after poem. The evidence for Yeats's existence in the midst of chaos in the last collection has become the tower. 'Meditations in Time of Civil War' establishes the tower with its surroundings and contents as symbol.

Events, lives and deaths whirl through these poems as Yeats, in his tower, at the centre of a turning world, sees the cruelty and atrocity of war rage around him, and relates events to larger patterns, the beginnings and endings of cycles – the rape of Leda by Zeus, initiating the change from one 2000-year cycle to another, the Christian annunciation and others.

The work of synthesis continues in 'Among Schoolchildren' in which the elder statesman and the passionate youth, the lover and the philosopher are seen as one organic whole. One of the images of this synthesis is that 'great-rooted blossomer' the chestnut tree: 'Are you the leaf, the blossom or the bole?' ('Among Schoolchildren'). Another is the fusion of dancer and dance.

The Winding Stair

The Winding Stair is, in many ways, a balancing of *The Tower*, as hinted earlier. You will notice that some of the poems in one collection have a form of counterpart in the other: 'Sailing to Byzantium' and 'Byzantium', for example, or 'A Man Young and Old' and 'A Woman Young and Old'. It seems that while in *The Tower* there is a drawing together, a defence, almost against the world outside, the poems in *The Winding Stair* are more inclusive. The physicality of the 'Crazy Jane' poems is an example, as is the marvellous section in 'Vacillations' when Yeats recalls sitting in a London café, an empty cup and his book on the table in front of him, and felt:

> *My body of a sudden blazed;*
> *And twenty minutes more or less*
> *It seemed so great my happiness*
> *That I was blessed and could bless.*

This and subsequent collections were written at a time when Yeats was suffering from a series of illnesses and was frequently abroad, recuperating. The themes continue to be explored, including those which will draw little sympathy from modern readers, such as the awfulness of 'the mob' and the middle classes, the superiority of the disinterested aristocracy on the one hand, and the noble peasant on the other. It might help here to remember that, in 1927, Lady Gregory had been made to sell Coole Park to the Forestry Department. The eighteenth century is held up as the antithesis to modern Ireland, a time when great men such as Swift, Berkeley and Burke stood for imagination over science and hated what Yeats called Whiggery, equating the rational and levelling with the rancorous.

Last Years, Last Poems

In the three decades before Yeats's death, some of his finest poems were written. If you have the *Everyman* edition, you will have the collection of poems which were published in 1938 and which were carefully organized by Yeats, under the heading 'New Poems', while the remaining poems, published after his death, are collected as 'Last Poems'. In the 1933 edition, all these poems are grouped under the title 'Last Poems'.

The headiness seen in *The Winding Stair* continues as the poet contemplates the historical gyres whirling and reflects that 'we that look on but laugh in tragic joy', freed by art to observe and also be part of the forces which shape us and our history:

> *In ancient tombs I sighed, but not again;*
> *What matter? Out of a cavern came a voice,*
> *And all it knows is that one word 'Rejoice'.*
>
> 'The Gyres'

The themes of the end of civilizations and the rise of new ones, the closeness of Yeats's own age to the end of its time are continued in 'Lapis Lazuli', while tragic heroes and heroines from Shakespeare are put into juxtaposition with historical figures such as King William IV and Kaiser Wilhelm. The 'hysterical women' who put politics and current affairs before art are swept uncontrollably up into the storm, not realizing, as Yeats has, that it is art which would enable them to understand,

> *All things fall and are built again*
> *And those that build them again are gay.*
> 'Lapis Lazuli'

This apparent detachment, however, is not easy to sustain and in 'An Acre of Grass', Yeats prays for 'an old man's frenzy', needing to shake himself free from contemplation to find the strength and passion necessary for writing poems. Figures from Irish history appear in a series of poems ranging from his indignation at the alleged forging of diaries used to convict Roger Casement, to Cromwell and the followers of Parnell, all told in the style of folk ballads, aligning modern heroes – and villains – with figures from folklore, while figures from Yeats's life are glimpsed in tableaux which capture their essences and place them among 'All the Olympians; a thing never known again'. ('Beautiful Lofty Things'). Yeats is, in these poems, creating myths from history. In 'The Municipal Gallery Revisited', he looks around the walls at 'the images of thirty years', selfless men who served the greater good of Ireland, the people who shaped him and his art. He invites his readers to visit the gallery, to see for ourselves and:

> *Think where man's glory most begins and ends,*
> *and say my glory was I had such friends.*

Maud Gonne is seen for the last time in 'A Bronze Head' as Yeats looks at the bust of her displayed in the gallery. He wonders how the beautiful woman could have become 'withered and mummy-dead', and contrasts the 'form all full/As though with magnanimity of light' with the form in front of him.

These last poems, revisiting people, places, styles and themes, have the air of a valediction and finish with 'Under Ben Bulben', which was visualized by Yeats as the poem which should close the final edition of his collected works. It sets out what he believes as he returns to his homeland, Sligo and his forefathers. It also provides an epitaph:

> *Cast a cold eye*
> *On life, on death,*
> *Horseman, pass by!*

✳ ✳ ✳ SUMMARY ✳ ✳ ✳

- The order of poems in each collection is deliberate and important.

- Collections complement each other. Watch for links, connections and echoes across them.

- Important themes are established in the early work, poetry, prose and drama.

- Early collections of lyric poetry represent attempts to find a right path.

- The symbol of the rose becomes dominant.

- *In The Seven Woods* marks the beginning of a change in tone, style and subject matter.

- *The Green Helmet* sees Yeats writing about himself in the public arena.

- *Responsibilities* can be read as a re-evaluation, a summing up.

- Yeats begins his autobiographical writings in 1917.

- The collections after 1917 draw heavily upon the system of gyres, wheels and cycles expounded in *A Vision*.

- The last poems revisit and reflect upon all that has gone before, from a new perspective and with new insight.

6 Contemporary Criticism

Yeats's work, as said before, is best considered as an organic whole and, as the survey of his major works shows, the canon is united by repeated themes, images and ideas, by developing philosophies and, not least, by the life of the poet from the love-lorn idealist of the early poems to the passionate old man of the last.

Criticism of Yeats's work during his lifetime is, therefore, criticism of a work in progress, and although some, such as Edmund Wilson, showed appreciation of what Yeats was doing, much of it is what Elizabeth Cullingford calls 'interesting now only as a warning of the dangers of premature judgement' (Elizabeth Cullingford, *Introduction to Yeats: Poems 1919–1935*, Macmillan, 1984).

Later criticism which was able to read across the whole, dealt with the various issues raised by Yeats and his work: his politics, his occult ideas, his personality, the system which informed his later work and his purposes, as well as the poetry, plays and prose themselves. Here was the main difficulty for someone trying to offer a criticism of Yeats's writing – where to start? What focus to take?

PRACTICAL AND NEW CRITICISM

'Practical Criticism' came to the fore in the 1920s to replace what its instigators saw as the woolly, subjective thinking about literature which had preceded it, with something more rigorous and analytical. What came to be called the Cambridge School of Critics, among them I.A. Richards, William Empson and F.R. Leavis, advocated a study of works of literature on their own terms rather than in terms of the author's intention, the effect on the reader or the sociological and biographical factors within which they were produced. Richards's 'Principles of Literary Criticism' worked towards providing a set of principles by which, and a vocabulary in which, literature could be properly evaluated. An American movement now referred to as 'New Criticism' followed a similar path, stressing what it called the 'autonomy' of the text, saying that the important thing in criticism is the text alone, what it has to say and how it communicates.

This view of literary criticism dominated until the 1970s, when new theories and methods became adopted by universities. It still implicitly informs much of the current work done for GCSE and A Level, where the text is still subject to what 'New Criticism' called 'close reading' – a critical examination to determine what it is saying and the effects it uses to communicate. The element expounded mainly by Leavis, that great literature promotes moral and cultural values, which it is the business of education to inculcate, has, however, greatly diminished.

CRITICISM: 1930s–1960s
After Yeats's death and with the wider availability of the collected poems and plays, there was tremendous critical interest and eventually division into a multitude of specialisms on different aspects of the poet's work. It is obvious that Yeats, with his emphasis on unity, cannot have been easy for the new and practical critics. Individual poems can, of course, be subject to the analysis of close criticism, but full appreciation comes within the context of the other poems and the factors that unify them.

MODERNISM
Modernism is the movement which, in all artistic fields, shaped the view of art held in the first two-thirds of the twentieth century. It shifted the emphasis away from the representational towards the subjective and impressionistic. The focus was no longer what was seen, but how it was seen: the presentation of the artist's vision of the object, rather than the object itself. It took novels away from the

KEYWORD

Modernism: in literature, a broad movement of writers, including T.S. Eliot, Pound, Joyce, Woolf, Yeats and D.H. Lawrence. Modernism was characterized by a persistent experimentation with language and form. Stream of consciousness is one of its major techniques, as well as dependence upon poetic image and myth.

omnipresent narrator who would relate and interpret event and character for us, dictating our responses and viewpoints, for example, as Henry Fielding does throughout *Tom Jones*, or as Victorian novelists do. It gave licence for less conventional forms of approach, allowing poets to use tones and cadences which are more like speech or prose, and allowing prose writers to be more flexible in the ways in which they used language.

Yeats began writing using the conventions of the nineteenth century, but adapted with enthusiasm to the underlying artistic philosophies of the twentieth century. A good illustration of this is to be found by reading a poem from the 1890s, say, from *The Rose*, and then turning at random to a poem from *The Tower* of 1928 and noting the differences, from 'We who are old, old and gay, O so old!' ('A Faery Song') to 'This is no country for old men' ('Sailing to Byzantium'). Modernism allowed writers to break with convention and find new voices, to write in free verse, to use non-chronological narratives and to employ stream of consciousness – it was a liberation from tradition and Yeats embraced it.

F.R. LEAVIS AND T.S. ELIOT

Leavis, in the 1932 *New Bearings in English Poetry*, describes Yeats's work, however praiseworthy he finds some of it, as, 'little more than a marginal comment on the main activities of his life'. His essay 'Yeats and the Nineteenth Century Tradition' takes Yeats's adoption of idiomatic, speech-like rhythms and dictions in favour of those of the Victorian period and, while Leavis praises the 'difficult and delicate sincerity', the 'extraordinarily subtle poise' of the later work, recognizing that Yeats has, as he intended, lost the 'conventional language' of fin de siècle poetry, believes that the attitudes which informed it have not gone. Yeats's insistence on symbol, concludes Leavis, comes from 'an unfortunate habit of mind' (F.R. Leavis, *New Bearings in English Poetry*, Penguin, 1960).

T.S. Eliot, however, despite being unsympathetic to some of Yeats's ideas and finding some of his expression unpleasant, treats the poetry and the plays together, finding each illuminating the other. He sees the emotion and passion of the early poetry and the recording of the intense experiences of youth expressed more forcefully in the later poetry, recognizing in the maturing style, the developing ideas, the perspective of middle age, a universality which makes Yeats a great poet: 'in beginning to speak as a particular man, he is beginning to speak for all men' ((T.S. Eliot in *Yeats: Poems, 1919–1935*, Cullingford (ed.), Macmillan, 1984).

RICHARD ELLMAN

The American writer and academic Richard Ellman is probably the most important of Yeats's critics and his two books, *Yeats: The Man and the Masks* (Penguin, 1979) and *The Identity of Yeats* (Macmillan, 1954) are essential reading. *The Man and the Masks* is a critical biography, taking us chronologically through Yeats's life and showing how Yeats's ideas were conceived and how they develop. Yeats's explanation of the doctrine of the masks and account of its application in various contexts is fascinating, and he sees Yeats's conscious projection of aspects of himself through fictional characters occurring as early as *John Sherman*, with Sherman and Howard representing dreamer and man of action as Robartes and Aherne would do later. Ellman believes that the three journeys in 'The Wanderings of Oisin' as depicting symbolically the three main phases of Yeats's early life spent in Sligo, Dublin and London, and he draws some interesting parallels, as well as giving insight to the relationship between Yeats and his father, and the effect of it upon the work.

The Identity of Yeats is more a collection of critical and expositional essays on aspects of Yeats's writing, including a lucid explanation of the systems in *A Vision*. Ellman writes that 'having all Yeats's poems before us is in itself a guide to reading them', and treats the work as an integrated whole, as well as offering approaches to individual poems in a very useful appendix. Compare F.R. Leavis's comments about symbolism in Yeats with this from Ellman:

> Beyond theme, symbol and style is the general patters or framework of Yeats's verse, in which each of these participates. Every poem embodies a schematisation, conscious as well as unconscious, of his way of living and seeing; and all his poems form a larger scheme which we can watch in the process of evolving.
>
> Richard Ellman, *The Identity of Yeats*, Macmillan, 1954

GEORGE ORWELL

Reviewing a 1943 biography of Yeats by V.K. Narayana Menon, George Orwell discusses Yeats's politics, and declares unequivocally, 'Translated into political terms, Yeats's tendency is fascist'. Orwell sees Yeats's hatred of all the factors in the modern world which will conspire to democratize it: science; mechanization and political movements. Yeats is not a believer in equality, but rather in a class system similar to that admired in seventeenth-century writing – the different nobilities of the aristocrat and the peasant, with the rest grubbing around for money, material well-being and self-importance in the middle. Orwell describes much of Yeats's imagery as 'feudal' and shows how his 'ordinary snobbishness' and authoritarian inclinations moved him towards his brief flirtation with Fascist parties. Orwell, interestingly, describes Yeats as 'too big a man to share the illusions of Liberalism', lacking the foresight to see that 'the new authoritarian civilisation, if it arrives, will not be aristocratic, or what he means by aristocratic' but ruled by, 'anonymous millionaires, shiny-bottomed bureaucrats and murdering gangsters'. Orwell's closing assertion is that the political and religious beliefs of a writer are far from incidental, but will 'leave their mark even on the smallest detail of his work' (George Orwell; review article included in *The Collected Essays, Journalism and Letters of George Orwell*, Sonia Orwell (ed.) and Ian Angus, Penguin, 1968).

W.H. AUDEN

The arguments about Yeats are brilliantly summarized in an article by
W.H. Auden entitled 'Prosecution and Defence' in which, taking the
roles of both attorneys, Auden sets out the prevailing attitudes.
Recognizing that 'the deceased had talent is not for a moment in
dispute', the prosecution categorizes Yeats as a dilettante, his 'feudal
mentality' leading hypocritically to extol the 'virtues of the peasant'
while himself seeking 'the world of the rich and decorative'. Auden
notes the 'singular moderation' with which Yeats supported a free
Ireland, writing, in 'Easter 1916' a poem which 'could offend neither
the Irish Republicans nor the British Army'. The prosecution's last
point, of course, cites the early belief in 'fairies' and the later belief in
'mumbo-jumbo'.

The defence begins by acknowledging that these views of Yeats's
character may or may not be true, but whether or not they 'prove
anything about the value of his poetry' is another matter. Yeats is
praised as a poet who reacted passionately to the world and, the
defence argues, 'the nature of that reaction matters very little'. The
relationship between art and society and the artist and history is
explored, leading to this conclusion:

... there is one field in which the poet is a man of action, the field of language, and it is precisely in this that the greatness of the deceased is most obviously shown. However false or undemocratic his ideas, his diction shows a continuous evolution towards what one might call the true democratic style.

> W.H. Auden, *The Public v. the Late Mr. William Butler Yeats*,
> 1939, quoted in *Yeats: Poems 1919–1935*, Cullingford, (ed.),
> Macmillan, 1984

GENERAL TONE

In his article of 1939, W.H. Auden encapsulated much of the ways of thinking about W.B. Yeats at that time. The plea to look at the poetry as well as the ideas was timely. It can be seen from the above, that criticism could, and did, focus on different aspects of Yeats's work – religion, politics, ideas – with the attendant danger that reaction to any one of these elements might dictate reaction to the poetry. In a similar way and more recently, reactions to a biography of and letters by Philip Larkin may have made some think him a lesser poet. Even Richard Ellman, who certainly sees the magnitude of Yeats's scope, will dismiss aspects of his thoughts and life, such as Yeats's eagerness to find aristocratic connections in his own family tree, as 'silly'. This word is used also by a very unsympathetic critic, Yvor Winters, who writes of Yeats, 'the better one understands him, the harder it is to take him seriously' (Yvor Winters, *Yeats's Silly Ideas*, reproduced in *Yeats: Poems 1919–1935*, Cullingford, (ed.), Macmilan, 1984).

In 1942, Alan Tate wrote an essay 'How Yeats Will Be Studied' in which he foresees the pending boom in specialist studies, fearing that the 'coming generation is likely to overdo the scholarly procedure' and lose the essence in the process (Alan Tate, 'How Yeats Will Be Studied', 1942, ibid).

This opinion proved to be justified as academics and critics began to specialize in different aspects of Yeats's work, some focusing on the autobiographical aspects, some offering analysis of the occult influences, others writing about Yeats's politics, still others specializing in his attitude to Ireland. Alan Tate seems almost to be anticipating the rise of literary theory and an approach to literature that does not necessarily take literature as its starting point.

* * * *SUMMARY* * * *

- Critics writing during Yeats's lifetime were, in effect, writing about work in progress.

- Of those critics writing shortly after Yeats's death, only a few understood his purpose.

- Early criticism often allows reaction to Yeats's ideas or personality to obstruct proper judgement of his poetry.

- It was anticipated by some that approaches to Yeats were likely to become so specialized and abstruse that his essence would be lost.

7 Modern Criticism

BACKGROUND

'Practical Criticism', with its emphasis on close reading and the autonomy of the text was challenged in the 1970s by the rise of what has become known by the generic term 'Literary Theory', which seeks in various ways to put texts back into contexts from within which they can be analysed and discussed. Both approaches offer a means of understanding and evaluating literature. Broadly speaking, one starts with the text, the other with the context.

Many believe that Literary Theory is a discipline in its own right, a broader structure than mere literary criticism. They think that any study of literature should begin with a study of theory, giving the reader contexts in which to read, and perspectives from which to approach, the texts. Theory raises important questions about historical, political, sexual, **semiological**, sociological and other contexts in which texts are written and the factors external to the author which influence the content or structure of the texts.

> ## KEYWORD
>
> Semiology: the science of signs and signals: semiotics is the study of the way in which they function. In linguistics, the Swiss theorist de Saussure drew a distinction between two elements in words: the signifier (the appearance or sound of the word) and the signified (the meaning to which the sign refers).

Literary Theory also raises questions about psychological factors internal to the author which might affect the content and the structure of the texts. It recognizes that the author may not be consciously aware of these influences and that the text is, therefore, partly written by influences of which the author is unaware. It is perhaps significant that, whereas the architects of Practical and New Criticism had their backgrounds in the study of English as a discipline, most of the architects of Theory are linguists, philosophers, sociologists and psychologists.

Literary Theory has also broadened the concept of what a text is, not confining its techniques of analysis to literary writings, such as plays, poems and novels. The old controversy about what we mean by 'literature' is, to some extent, irrelevant: everything written, filmed, painted or presented, which needs interpretation by a reader or viewer is deemed to be text. This is now reflected in public examinations in English where pupils are required to comment on and analyse not only poems by Ted Hughes or Seamus Heaney, but also newspaper articles, advertisements and charity leaflets.

A COMPARISON

An idea of the broad differences between older and newer schools of criticism might be given by looking at Yvor Winters's account of a particular poem, 'Leda and the Swan', written in 1960 (*Yeats's Silly Ideas*, included in *Yeats's Poems, 1919–1935*, Elizabeth Cullingord, (ed.), Macmillan, 1984, pages 123–30), and the approach taken to it by Wilhelm Johnsen 30 years later (*Textual/Sexual Politics in Yeats's Leda and the Swan*, included in *Yeats and Post-modernism*, Leonard Orr, (ed.), Syracuse University Press, 1991, pages 80-8).

Yvor Winters summarizes the story of the poem straightforwardly as an account of the rape of Leda by Zeus, in the form of a swan, an act of violence which led, via the birth of Helen and the destruction of Troy, to the collapse of one cycle of Greek civilization and the rise of another. Winters concedes that the rape is 'impressively' written, but is of the opinion that, 'an account of a rape in itself has very limited possibilities in poetry'. The important thing in this poem is that the rape is of a mortal by an immortal. In this, he says, lies either the power or the weakness of the poem. This opening clearly shows that the critic intends to examine the poem in front of him, its expression of the writer's ideas, and the validity or otherwise of those ideas.

Wilhelm Johnsen's summary of the content of the poem is shorter: 'Leda and the Swan', he says, is 'depicting a rape as the welcome sign of a better future'. Where Winters's summary tells us what the poem is about in the most basic sense, Johnsen's suggests a point of view, an interpretation, a discussion of attitudes and assumptions in and beyond the poem. He immediately draws attention to the paradox of a good rape.

Yvor Winters's criticism is not a flattering one: he does not like the fact that he has to go beyond the poem to appreciate the significance of the cycles, particularly to a book such as *A Vision*, expounding theories 'which are, after all, ridiculous'. As does Johnsen, Winters looks at the ambiguities in the last lines of the poem and the possible answers to the questions posed there:

> *Did she put on his knowledge with the power,*
> *Before the indifferent beak could let her drop?*

Winters states possible interpretations, but does not examine them or pursue the implications of them, contenting himself with stating, once the possibilities have been numbered, 'I suspect the last, but would have difficulty proving it'.

Johnsen examines two versions of the poem, one, the poem which finally appeared in *The Tower* and the other an earlier draft. He shows, with detailed textual reference, the subtle changes made in the language to turn an act of annunciation with implicit compliance from Leda, to a brutal act of rape. For example, from the description of the bird 'hovering still', implying a settling, a coming to rest, to 'beating still', implying motion and in motion, force. In the first version the swan 'laid her helpless face' upon its breast, in the second, it 'held her helpless face' there. Johnsen looks at the ending and the meaning of the poem in the light of these changes.

Although he does look outside to the expression of similar ideas in other Yeats poems, Winters can find no basis for taking the poem seriously. He sees no harm in taking a Greek myth as the vehicle for the poem if 'the tenor is serious', but 'the tenor is a myth of Yeats's making, and is foolish'. In order to take the poem seriously, we must, he says, take all sorts of nonsense such as the 2000-year historical cycle and the equation of the sexual union with mystical experience seriously.

Johnsen starts with Yeats, intending a political reading of the poem, but finds politics soon swamped by 'bird and lady'. He continues, comparing different versions of the poem, looking at other references to the legend in mythology, contrasting 'the theoretical potential' of *A Vision* with 'poetic thinking', and referring to other critics in his examination of Yeats's statements about antithesis, offering an analysis of the poem based on Marxist and feminist readings.

OVER TO YOU

You need to think about your reactions to these two examples of critical technique. It will be apparent that Yvor Winters's practical criticism of Yeats is as much about himself as it is about Yeats, and also that you are not invited to disagree with Winters's ideas about Yeats's theories and systems. You will also notice that the critic deals with the poem, by and large, as a finite unit, and that he objects to having to go outside it to elucidate meaning, particularly when he holds what he has to look at in such contempt.

On the other hand, Winters takes the poem on Yeats's own terms, while the Literary Theorist, Johnsen, who ranges far away from the poet's conscious or expressed intentions, offers interpretations of purposes and meanings which Yeats might not recognize. The polarity is clear: the poet and the poem taken as self-contained, on their own merits and discussed by a knowledgeable critic, or the application of the poet's work to wider principles and circumstances, some of which the poet might not be conscious of, but which enables a reader to relate the poet and the work to wider issues.

CLOSE READING

Both Practical Criticism and Literary Theory require close reading and analysis, but the starting points for that close reading are often rather different. Let us consider William Empson's piece on Yeats's 'Who Goes With Fergus', written in 1930, with Kitti Carriker's essay 'The Doll as Icon', a semiotic analysis of Yeats's 'The Dolls' and 'Upon a Dying Lady'. Empson, in his book *Seven Types of Ambiguity* (1973), identifies the Fergus poem as an example of the sixth type of ambiguity, 'irrelevant statements', and refers to an earlier poem, 'Fergus and the Druid' in which King Fergus, tired of the active life, is given a bag of dreams by a Druid, awakens to the contemplative life and, finding that he has 'grown nothing, being all', cries:

> *Ah, Druid, Druid, how great webs of sorrow*
> *Lay hidden in the small slate-coloured thing.*

What follows is a close examination of the implications of the word 'now' in the line 'who will go with Fergus now?' and whether it means before or after the transformation recorded in 'Fergus and the Druid'. Empson unravels a whole skein of possible interpretations of subsequent lines.

Looking at the lines:

> *Young man, lift up your russet brow,*
> *And lift your tender eyelids, maid,*

And brood on hopes and fear no more
And no more turn aside and brood
Upon love's bitter mystery,
For Felix rules the brazen cars,

Empson notes that the poem seems to tell the man and maid not to brood, but that the tone is barely imperative, more of 'advice and personal statement', that statement expressing loss. Again, the syntax of the poem is used to explicate possible different interpretations. Empson concludes: 'The wavering and indefiniteness of nineteenth-century poetry is often merely weak. When, as here, it has a great deal of energy and sticks in your head, it is usually because the opposites are tied round a single strong idea' (William Empson, *Seven Types of Ambiguity*, Chatto and Windus, 1973, pages 187–90). Close analysis of a particular poem is used to make a general statement about the poetry of a particular age, but what is being discussed is always the poem.

Kitti Carriker begins her essay with an account of **Freud**'s identification of dolls as an example of things that can arouse in people a strong sense of 'the uncanny', brought about in this case by the miniaturization of the human form in idealized bodies, while recognizing that this sense of the uncanny does not proceed from infantile fears, as children have no fear of their dolls coming to life.

Unlike Empson, Carriker's starting point is outside the poems she will discuss, and she then works in. She describes 'The Dolls' as a poem about 'a dollmaker and the reaction of the dolls in his shop when a child is born to him and his wife'. She notes that the dolls, seeing themselves as rivals to the child, are 'simultaneously human and inhuman' and because of this are perceived

KEYWORD

Freudian criticism: this interprets literature in the same way that Freudian psychoanalysts interpret dreams – as a product of the subconscious in which repressed desires and censored thoughts are disguised and made acceptable, by being cloaked in symbol. The psychoanalytical critic will interpret words and images from a Freudian or post-Freudian viewpoint to find their real meanings in terms of the author's unconscious. It is a way of finding the psychological realities which inform art.

as uncanny. Carriker identifies the tension in the poem hinging on the question of whether or not the dolls are subject or object. The dolls see themselves as the subject because the arrival of the object, the child, threatens to displace them. For the dolls, who appear living and animate, it is the baby who is negative: 'noisy and filthy'. Carriker writes that in this poem, 'the dolls are icons – not the body-made-object but the body-made-subject (or more specifically, the object-made-subject by virtue of animation)' (Kitti Carriker, *The Doll as Icon*, included in *Yeats and Postmodernism*, Leonard Orr, (ed.), Syracuse University Press, 1991, pages 126–43). The dolls give a representation of the self which is unsettling, greeting the arrival of a child with jealousy and fear.

PSYCHOANALYTICAL FEMINIST CRITICISM

Because Yeats's work and life were so entwined as a matter of philosophy, because Yeats wrote about his life in memoirs and autobiographies as well as poems and because so many of Yeats's contemporaries wrote their own accounts of events, there is a wealth of material for the psychoanalytical critic to consider. Similarly, due to the fact that Yeats's relationships with women were so central to his poetry, so rife with ambiguity and because part of Yeats's method of presentation was to mythologize, to identify types, there is much for the **feminist critic** to consider as well.

Deirdre Toomey, in her essay 'Labyrinths' starts with the lines in the poem 'The Tower' where Yeats expresses shame at having turned aside 'from a great labyrinth', the memory of that shame having the effect that, even after a great deal of time, 'the sun's/Under eclipse and the day's blotted out'.

> **KEYWORD**
>
> Feminist criticism: this takes the view that male writers are unconsciously influenced by the predominant views about women and their place in society in the age in which they write, as well as being influenced by assumptions about women and 'the feminine' inherent in patriarchal societies. Feminist criticsim offers interpretations of texts that try to expose these attitudes and see how they work, locating assumptions hidden in the language used and showing how these assumptions affect the representation of women.

From the *Memoirs*, Toomey identifies the shame arising from incidents in December 1898. Maud Gonne had told Yeats of her relationship with Lucien Millevoye and that she had two children by him, one of which was Iseult, whom Yeats had previously assumed adopted. He had defended Maud Gonne against rumours which, he now learned, were justified. The previous day, the two had discussed dreams in which they had met and kissed and Maud Gonne told him that she had dreamed of being married to him by 'a great spirit'. Deirdre Toomey says that this dream is a 'revelation of an unconscious wish' and that Maud Gonne was signalling to Yeats that she was ready to marry him. Her confession to him of the paternity of her children was a sign of her trust.

The effect upon Yeats, however, was the opposite from what was intended or hoped. Toomey quotes Maud Gonne's perceptive interpretation of Yeats's response in her reply to a later proposal in 1902: 'you make beautiful poetry out of what you call your unhappiness, and you are happy in that. Marriage would be such a dull affair. Poets should never marry' (Deirdre Toomey, 'Labyrinths – Yeats and Maude Gonne' from *Yeats and Women*, Toomey, (ed.), Macmillan, 1997, page 6).

In 1898, however, when Maud Gonne was indicating her readiness to accept his proposal, Yeats did not make one. If this is the case, then the lines in 'The Tower' take on new significance. He turned aside, Yeats says,

> *out of pride,*
> *Cowardice, some silly over-subtle thought*
> *Or anything called conscience once.*

These are the events of 1898 powerfully recalled among the 'images and memories' in 1928, the shame of the recollection still burning. Deirdre Toomey takes this as the reason why Yeats wrote no new poetry for over a year from 1898, why he began the revising of some of his work in production, and why his work on the Celtic Mystical Order became more intense over the two years following these events: 'a substitute both for the writing of poetry and … for any sexual relationship with Maud Gonne'. On another level, the revelations and Yeats's reaction to them had rendered poems concerned with Maud Gonne and his image of her false, and Toomey shows how Yeats's perception and presentation of Maud Gonne had to be 'radically reconstructed'. Yeats needed the safety of unrequited love, the tension that frustration and yearning caused and that was necessary to the poetry. Vividly, Toomey sums up Yeats's position: 'Maud Gonne did call Willie's bluff in 1898; that is, she violated the security of his frustration'. She showed him that she was a sexual creature, 'thus destroying the elaborate polarities of *A Wind Among the Reeds*'.

This premise leads to a fascinating reassessment of Yeats's presentation of Maud Gonne in later poems when, in middle age and as an old man, Yeats, in a sort of 'delayed reaction', remembers and relives with new insight the passions of his youth, detecting undercurrents of 'guilt and self-condemnation' in some of the poems, of 'blame and accusation', and even, in 'Against Uncertain Praise' (1910) identifying himself with the 'knaves and dolts ... who have misjudged or exploited Maud Gonne's idealism'. Toomey shows how, in poems such as 'A Thought for Propertius', Yeats continues to try to come to terms with two Maud Gonnes: the sexual being and the heroic virgin of his mythology.

Toomey analyses the significance of the labyrinth in Yeats's imagery. She gives its conventional meaning in the poem 'Against Unworthy Praise' as a reflection of the secrets and mysteries of Maud Gonne's life. However, by considering the history of the labyrinth in mythology, Toomey shows that a distinction is drawn between the imagery of the labyrinth when applied to males – artistic – and when applied to women – sexual degradation. From this viewpoint, Toomey examines 'A Thought for Propertius', detecting a remaining horror at Maud Gonne's sexuality 'encoded in the image of the labyrinth'. Citing a feminist psychoanalyst, Toomey detects elements of 'a universal male fear of women' which man tries to rid himself of by objectification (Deirdre Toomey '*Labyrinths: Yeats and Maud Gonne*' from *Yeats and Women*, Toomey, (ed.), Macmillan, 1997).

POLITICS

An assessment of Yeats as an 'indisputable great national poet who articulates the experiences, the aspirations and the vision of people suffering under the dominion of an off-shore power' seeks to move beyond a 'crudely political reading', presumably such as that offered by Orwell in 1943. Edward Said, in his essay, 'Yeats and Decolonization' argues for this interpretation of Yeats and sees him in the broader context of a colonial world governed by European imperialism (Edward Said, 'Yeats and Decolonization' from *Literature in the Modern World*, Dennis Walder, (ed.), Oxford University Press, 1990, pages 34–41).

Said states that much of the resistance to colonization and imperialism is conducted in the name of nationalism, the desire to mobilize resistance to an occupying power in the name of a different cultural, historical, religious, linguistic experience from which the colonizers are excluded and that they have suppressed. Nationalism carries with it the danger, however, that the colonial power, once gone, will be replaced by another power which, although representing the culture which it has sought to free, nonetheless 'gets the old colonial structure replicated in new national terms'. As Yeats put it, 'the beggars have changed places, but the lash goes on' ('The Great Day').

Said also argues that a weakness of nationalism is that there is so much of the colonizer in the colonized. The period of colonization represents almost a shared history, the values, systems and ideologies of the colonizers are introduced through the institutions set up by them, from schools to railway systems to legal systems. He says 'imperialism is a co-operative venture'. This has the effect of humanizing the colonizer and, at the same time, emphasizing the divide between 'native and Westerner'.

Edward Said identifies two defining moments in nationalist revivals: the first, a recognition that the colonizing culture is imperialist; the second, the desire for liberation from it. There is 'a pressing need for recovery of the land', and, with it, the search for an identity independent of the colonial history, something indigenous, authentic and national. Along with this, comes a revival of the language.

Said sees Yeats's writing as fitting that pattern of resistance or renovation, from the early preoccupations with Irish folk stories and themes, to the later years when Yeats laboured at constructing systems, ways of interpreting history and defining the future. Yeats was aware of the tension that existed between his own nationalism and the English cultural heritage, embodied in Lady Gregory and Coole Park which he so admired. Said speculates that it is this 'urgently political and secular tension' which 'caused him to try and resolve it on a higher, that is, non-political level' – the level of the universal, the occult.

Placing Yeats in a broader context of occupation and liberation allows Said to consider the claims of other critics. Those aspects of Yeats's thought which seemed to them ridiculous and repellent – his, for want of a better word, snobbery; his authoritarianism; his fascination with the occult – could be interpreted differently, as part of Yeats's search for a 'national signature' and his rage at those who, in his eyes, would compromise it.

If this interpretation holds, when we read poems in which Yeats's thoughts strike us as scathing and contemptuous of people of whom he disapproves, we are really seeing the frustration of a poet who is trying 'to announce the contours of an ideal community, crystallized not only by its sense of itself but also by its enemy'. Yeats's system saw history in terms of cycles, seeing each new cycle ushered in by an act of violence – the rape of Leda; the 'blood-dimmed tide' of 'The Second Coming'. One of Yeats's great themes, Said says, is 'how to reconcile the inevitable violence of the colonial conflict with the everyday politics of an ongoing national struggle, and also with the power of each of the various parties in the colonial conflict, with the discourse of reason, of persuasion, of organisation, with the requirements of poetry'. Yeats is saying that more than violence is needed, and that liberation is about more than simply seizing power.

VIEWS OF HISTORY

Ways in which writers and their works can be revisited and reinterpreted in the light of later insights and philosophies can be found in the practices of **historicism**. In his essay sub-titled 'Yeats and the Tropics of History', William Bonney draws upon the thinking of theorists such as Hayden White and Morse Peckham to offer an evaluation of Yeats's presentation of history, concentrating upon 'Easter Rising 1916' and 'Coole Park and Ballylee 1931' (William Bonney, 'He Liked the Way His Finger Smelt: Yeats and the Tropics of History', from *Yeats and Post-Modernism*, Leonard Orr, (ed.), Syracuse University Press, 1991).

> **KEYWORD**
>
> Historicism/New historicism: these schools of thought consider texts in close relation to the historical contexts in which they were written. They can examine literary texts in conjunction with other contemporary, non-literary, writing, looking at the cultural, religious and other factors which underpinned the production of literature. They will also challenge notions of the nature of history, historical writing and our perceptions of history.

Bonney begins his essay with an account of how views of history have changed. He represents traditional historians as those who assume that 'historical narratives are verbal structures' able to reveal facts and stories, presenting them as corresponding to 'some prior but recoverable empirical reality'. Poets such as Yeats and Wordsworth, with their 'perceptions of the ultimately subjective essence of the historical process and of human access to vestiges of this process' have been, therefore, denied acknowledgement as historians. The gradual recognition that the notion of history in itself causes problems because the word 'history' refers both 'to an object of knowledge and to an exploratory analysis of this object' means that the concept of an historical fact or a single event which took place in history has been challenged. An historical fact is as much a matter of interpretation as any other.

Leading on from this point, Bonney presents Hayden White's view that historical narratives are 'verbal fictions, the contents of which are as much invented as found'. They may be seen as extended metaphors which correspond to those used in literature. The notion of historical narrative as a kind of extended metaphor leads us to the idea of **tropes** and an examination of the trope of **irony**.

With the hitherto presumed difference between objective fact and subjective impression removed, or at least blurred, a re-evaluation of Yeats's writing about his times and the events he lived through becomes possible. Bonney notes that Yeats is well aware of the fact that human perception can only be expressed through language and that language introduces its own ambiguous, contradictory and unstable elements. Any idea of a progression through time is ironic and his own perceptions and definitions, therefore, are open to question. Figurative language is the province of the poet and these ironies are best expressed, not in language which strives for an unachievable objectivity, but in poetic structures. Yeats's concern with patterns and cycles reveals a recognition that behind events there is a continuous structure of relationships and a continual return of 'the Same in the Different'.

> **KEYWORDS**
>
> Trope: essentially figurative language, but carrying the sense that the departure from ordinary speech is as much a matter of syntax and tone as of image.
>
> Irony: simply put, a way of saying one thing while meaning another. This definition has been expanded to include literature which presents a variety of possible views about its subject matter, or which shows an awareness of many possible points of view.

Bonney finds Yeats 'disoriented and dismayed by specific events of contemporary history, in spite of his repeated affirmation of general and inclusive tidiness.' Bonney explores this trope, this irony, and finds it to be 'tropological inconsistency' which is dealt with in 'unrewarding skirmishes'. In both 'Coole Park and Ballylee 1931' and 'Easter 1916', for example, 'a contemplative toil is dramatized with conceptual alternatives as a persona tries to reconcile destructive temporality with a desire for continuity.' But one poem deals with a personal and essentially tragic sense of time passing, while the other tries to find reasons to believe that the Easter rebellion has lasting significance.

Both poems employ the image of a stream to represent the flux and flow of time and events, but in one it shows 'the anxiety engendered by the terrors of time within the mind of a thoughtful and troubled, if feckless, narrator', while in the other it 'seeks to accomplish a compensatory, perhaps even redemptive, orientation towards public slaughter.' Presenting the temporal flux at times as tragic and troubling and at others as joyous and to be celebrated is a trope which, for Bonney, is not reconciled in Yeats and causes many problems. 'He at last seems to be suggesting that decisions to conceive of the temporal flux as mournful or joyous, tragic or comic, are never final or concordant, and thus are only to be made ironically.'

✳ ✳ ✳ *SUMMARY* ✳ ✳ ✳

- Literary Theory often starts at points which are outside the text and uses the text to illustrate political, historical, sociological, linguistic and other issues.

- Many think that Theory should be studied before being applied to literary texts.

- Theory deals with literary texts in wider contexts and relates them to contemporary philosophies or wider themes.

- There are various schools of Theory, each of which has its own approaches and ideas.

- Wide reading beyond the text that you are studying may be necessary.

8 Where to Next?

It is hoped that this short introduction will make you want to explore Yeats's writing further. Depending upon which of the many aspects of Yeats's life and work has caught your interest, here are some suggestions for further reading. More titles can be found in the Further Reading section.

These suggestions represent only a fraction of what has been written about Yeats. In this book recommendations have been confined to books that are relatively easy to find in libraries, high-street bookshops, second-hand bookshops, through book-searches or on the internet.

SOURCES

The 1933 *Collected Poems* and the *Everyman* edition of the poems are easy to find. For Yeats's fiction, there is an excellent collection in Penguin, edited by G.J. Watson under the title *Short Fiction*. Very helpful also is a collection called *The Major Works* edited by Edward Larrissey, containing samples of all genres: poems; plays; senate speeches; essays; letters; fiction and autobiography. Other titles are published by Macmillan.

BIOGRAPHY

There are several good biographies which will give you more background information about Yeats's life and times, relating and speculating upon the circumstances which gave rise to ideas, poems, plays, etc. There are, of course, Yeats's own accounts to be found in *Memoirs* and *Autobiographies*.

Richard Ellman's *Yeats: The Man and the Masks* is, perhaps, the seminal work. Beginning with accounts of the author's interviews with Mrs Yeats and with Maud Gonne MacBride, this is a pioneering work, entertaining, accessible, full of insight in its acknowledgment of the scope and importance of Yeats's work. Brenda Maddox's *Georgie's Ghosts* concentrates upon Yeats's relationship with his wife and her automatic writing, drawing upon material that was not made available until 1992. *W.B. Yeats: A Life* by Stephen Coote, written in 1997, is a thorough account of Yeats's life and works, again drawing upon new material and with some interesting insights and speculations. Letters are also available in a growing edition of the collected letters, or in various one-volume editions, including the letters between Yeats and Maud Gonne: *Always Your Friend: The Gonne-Yeats Letters 1893–1938*, edited by A. Norman Jeffares and Anna Macbride.

COMMENTARY

If you have received an impression of the main ideas and themes of Yeats's work as well as some sense of its cohesiveness and organization, you will want to read further and more deeply with the help of commentaries to assist you.

The standard work is A. Norman Jeffares's *A New Commentary on the Poems of W.B. Yeats*. The excellent Everyman edition of *The Poems*, edited by Daniel Albright, contains thorough and clear glossaries of and notes upon all the poems which, as Albright says in his introduction, draw upon Jeffares, but supplement him with the latest scholarship. John Unterecker's *A Reader's Guide to W.B. Yeats* is a clear, thorough and lively commentary on all the poems in the order that they appear in the 1933 edition, and is well worth studying, as is Nicholas Drake's *The Poetry of W.B. Yeats*.

Pursuing the plays is rather more difficult since, of course, there is the question of staging and performance. Very useful, therefore, is Richard Taylor's *A Reader's Guide to the Plays of W.B. Yeats* which not only discusses narrative and theme, but also describes how the plays were to be presented on stage, often looking at changes made by Yeats during or between productions. It also contains clear accounts of masks, symbols and magic and their application to the plays.

CRITICISM: GENERAL

The critical works of earlier generations of critics are always worth reading, not only for their insights and erudition, but also for their style, wit and sense of engagement with the text. Essays by T.S. Eliot, William Empson, F.R. Leavis, I.A. Richards and others are readily available and there are two very good compilations of critical responses edited by Elizabeth Cullingford and John Stallworthy. Vital is Richard Ellman's *The Identity of Yeats*.

Literary Theory, starting as it often does outside the text, needs to be approached more circumspectly. There are many introductions to Theory on the market and particularly useful are Terry Eagleton's *Literary Theory* and *Beginning Theory* by Peter Barry. The former is a survey, the latter is illustrated with examples of approaches and tips about how to get into them, plus some practical exercises. A good collection of essays on various subjects showing the diversity of Theory is *Literature in the Modern World* edited by Dennis Walder, which contains the essay by Edward Said, 'Yeats and Decolonization'.

SPECIFIC CRITICISM

Practical Criticism, starting as it does with the text and dealing with the text in its own terms, is easy and entertaining to read, rather like entering into a dialogue with someone else who has read the books. Literary Theory, however, is not always so accessible, often taking as its starting point, theories expounded in journals or specialist works which are hard to find. This is why beginning with books such as those by Eagleton and Barry is so helpful. There is an excellent collection of essays edited by Deirdre Toomey called *Yeats and Women*, with essays on Maud Gonne, Olivia Shakespear and Lady Gregory, amongst others, and which concludes with a transcript of a radio broadcast on the subject of 'Poems About Women' given by Yeats in 1932. Of considerable interest also is *Yeats and Postmodernism*, edited by Leonard Orr, which contains a variety of approaches to poetry and plays.

OTHER INTERESTS

There is a great deal of specialization in Yeats's studies, not all of it easy to find and not all of it worth the struggle if you do find it. Of particular, if occasionally rarefied interest, are the following.

Yeats and the Beginnings of the Irish Renaissance by Philip A. Marcus concentrates on the period between 1885 and 1889, while clear accounts of occult matters are given in Kathleen Raine's *Yeats, the Tarot and the Golden Dawn,* and Helen Hennessy Vendler's *Yeats's Vision and the Later Plays.*

John Stallworthy's *Between the Lines* examines how some of the major works were constructed, using different drafts and re-drafts to show vividly a poet at work.

The Rhizome and the Flower by James Olney examines the similarities in thought and imagery between Yeats and Jung.

Each of the above books will yield bibliographies of their own and the scope for the pursuit of matters Yeatsian is virtually endless.

GLOSSARY

Archetype an original type; a first model; themes, images and characters which recur throughout myth and literature.

Ballad a poem which tells a story.

Canon the established body of work of an author.

elegy a lament on the death of a person.

Feminist criticism analysis of literature which, among other concerns, aims to show how perceptions of women prevalent in society can unconsciously influence an author's representation of women in a text, presenting them according to stereotypes or projected feminine qualities.

Fenian a movement which began in the late-eighteenth century in America and was named after the Fianna, warriors from Irish legend. It advocated the immediate overthrow of British rule in Ireland, by force if necessary.

Figurative language language which uses figures of speech, such as metaphor, to lend emphases of which everyday, literal language is incapable.

Freudian criticism analysis of literature which, among other concerns, aims to expose the hidden psychological influences upon the author that are hidden in the text

Historicism analysis of literature which, among other concerns, aims to find the historical influences that govern the writing and the context of a text and to see works of literature in historical context.

Imagery painting pictures in words, often pictures that carry connotations and meanings which the words alone are incapable of carrying.

Irony saying one thing while another is meant; consciously making many possible points of view and interpretations implicit in a text.

Linguistics the scientific study of language.

Lyrical poetry originally a song to be accompanied by the lyre; now any short poem on a personal subject or theme.

Metaphor a figure of speech; a way of describing one thing as another, allowing the consequent allusions to convey the qualities of the thing thus described.

Modernism in literature, a broad movement of writers including T.S. Eliot, Pound, Joyce, Woolf, W.B. Yeats and D.H. Lawrence. It was characterized by a persistent experimentation with language and form. Stream of consciousness is one of its major techniques as well as dependence upon poetic image and myth.

Satire literature which exposes vice or folly to laughter and contempt.

Semiology a science which studies the life of signs within a society.

Signified the meaning to which the signifier refers.

Signifier the simple appearance or sound of a word.

Symbol something which represents something else, generally by association or analogy.

Symbolist a late nineteenth-century movement in art and poetry which saw the actual world as a representation or expression of something else.

Themes ideas or concerns which permeate a writer's work.

Theosophy a generic term for mystical philosophies which say that a knowledge of God can be achieved through such means as direct intuition, spiritual ecstasy or a progression through rites and rituals.

Trope   figurative language in
which the order and effect of
words is employed as well as
visual imagery.

Wildean   in the manner of
Oscar Wilde, nineteenth-century
wit and dramatist, famous for his
prolific output of memorable
sayings, quips and put-downs.

FURTHER READING

Barry, Peter, *Beginning Theory*, Manchester, 1995

Coote, Stephen, *W.B. Yeats: A Life*, Hodder and Stoughton, 1997

Cullingford, Elizabeth (ed.), *Yeats: Poems 1919–1935*, Macmillan, 1984

Drake, Nicholas, *Poetry of W.B. Yeats*, Penguin, 1991

Eagleton, Terry, *Literary Theory*, Blackwell, 1983

Ellman, Richard, *Yeats: The Man and the Masks*, Penguin, 1987

Ellman, Richard, *The Identity of Yeats*, Macmillan, 1959

Empson, William, *Seven Types of Ambiguity*, Chatto and Windus, 1973

Gray, Michael, *Dictionary of Literary Terms*, Longman, 1992

Henn, T.R., *The Lonely Tower*, Methuen, 1965

Jeffares, A. Norman, *New Commentary on the Poems of W. B. Yeats*, Macmillan, 1984

Jeffares, A. Norman, *W.B.Yeats: The Critical Heritage*, Routledge and Kegan Paul, 1977

Leavis, F.R., *New Bearings in English Poetry*, Penguin, 1960

Macneice, Louis, *The Poetry of W B Yeats*, Oxford University Press, 1941

Maddox, Brenda, *Georgie's Ghosts*, Picador, 1999

Marcus, Philip L., *Yeats and the Beginning of the Irish Renaissance*, Cornell University Press, 1970

Olney, James, *The Rhizome and the Flower*, University of Chicago Press, 1980

Orr, Leonard (ed.), *Yeats and PostModernism*, Syracuse University Press, 1991

Raine, Kathleen, *Yeats, the Tarot and the Golden Dawn*, Dolmen, 1972

Rajan, Balachandra, *W.B. Yeats*, Hutchinson, 1965

Somerset-Fry, P. and F., *Short History of Ireland*, Routledge, 1991

Stallworthy, John, *Between the Lines*, Oxford University Press, 1963

Taylor, Richard, *Reader's Guide to the Plays of W B Yeats*, Macmillan, 1984

Toomey, Deirdre (ed.), *Yeats and Women*, Macmillan, 1992

Unterecker, John, *Reader's Guide to W.B. Yeats*, Thames and Hudson, 1975

Unterecker, John (ed.), *Yeats: A Collection of Critical Essays*, 1982

Vendler, Helen, *Yeats's Vision and the Later Plays*, Oxford University Press, 1973

Walder, Dennis (ed.), *Literature in the Modern World*, Oxford University Press, 1990

White and Jeffares (ed.), *The Gonne/Yeats Letters 1893–1938*, Pimlico, 1992

Yeats, W.B., *Collected Poems*, Macmillan, 1933

Yeats, W.B., *Major Works* (edited by Edward Larrissey), Oxford University Press, 1997

Yeats, W.B., *A Vision*, Macmillan, 1961

Yeats, W.B., *Autobiographies*, Macmillan, 1955

Yeats, W.B., *Mythologies*, Macmillan, 1952

Yeats, W.B., *The Poems* (edited by Daniel Albright), J M Dent, 1990

Yeats, W.B., *Memoirs*, (edited by Denis Donoghue), Macmillan, 1972

Yeats, W.B., *Short Fiction*, (edited by G.J. Watson), Penguin, 1995

Yeats, W.B., *Essays and Introductions*, Macmillan, 1961

INDEX